Where Do I Come In?

JOINING GOD'S MISSION

Brian Keepers

FAITH
ALIVE®
Christian Resources

Photo: iStock

This study is part of In the Works, a faith formation program for adults.

Studies in this series include:
Where Do I Come In? Joining God's Mission
What Do I Do with My Life? Serving God through Work
What Do I Owe? Managing the Gifts God Gives You
How Do I Make It Right? Doing Justice in a Broken World
How Do I Begin? Sharing Your Faith

Unless otherwise indicated, Scripture quotations in this publication are from the Holy Bible, New Revised Standard Version, ©1989, Division of Christian Education of the National Council of Churches of Christ in the United States of America. Used by permission.

We welcome your comments. Call us at 1-800-333-8300 or e-mail us at editors@faithaliveresources.org.

ISBN 978-1-59255-473-7

10 9 8 7 6 5 4 3 2 1

Contents

Week 4: Missional Improvisation

Week 5: Finding *Your Place* in the Story

How to Use This Book

Where Do I Come In? Joining God's Mission, as well as the other books in the In the Works series, offers a unique format that combines insightful daily devotions with a discussion guide for small groups. It's simple and easy to use. Here's all you need to do:

Before your group meeting, please carefully read the five daily readings that offer insights on the topic for the week. You'll find them stimulating and full of practical ways to help you join God's mission in the world. We suggest reading one devotional on each of the five days rather than reading through all five at once. That way you can take your time and reflect on what the reading says to you personally. You may want to highlight lines that speak to you or jot questions or comments in the margin.

Note: Before your first small group session, you should have received a copy of this book so you can read the daily readings for Week 1 prior to your first meeting.

During your group meeting, use the small group discussion guides found at the end of each week of readings. These self-directing guides offer plenty to talk about for forty-five minutes to an hour or more. Groups should feel free to use them selectively, choosing the questions or activities that fit the group and the amount of time you have.

Each discussion guide includes

- an **Opening** question or activity that takes group members into the topic for the session.
- a **Bible Study** of passages that relate to the topic of the week. Group members should bring their own Bibles to the meetings or arrange to have a supply of Bibles available.
- **Group Discussion** questions that take participants back into the daily readings for the week and help relate them to their daily lives. Groups should feel free to select which of these questions they want to discuss; of course, you can

always substitute questions and comments from group members for our precooked ones!

- a brief **Closing** time of focus and prayer.
- **Action Options** for groups and for individuals. These are suggestions for follow-up activities that flow from the daily readings and group discussion.

From time to time, the discussion guides offer **Options** or **Alternative Approaches**, giving groups a choice of activities or questions.

Of course you'll want someone who's willing to lead the discussion and keep things moving for each small group meeting. But the discussion guide is written for the whole group, not just the leader. Together, may you grow in your understanding of God's mission in the world as you consider your own place in it.

—Faith Alive staff

Introduction

One of my favorite books of all time is C. S. Lewis's *The Lion, the Witch and the Wardrobe*. Four children named Peter, Susan, Edmund, and Lucy are sent to the English countryside to live with Professor Digory Kirke during World War II. While exploring the professor's house, they stumble through an old wardrobe and discover the magical world of Narnia. But all is not well—Narnia is under the curse of the wicked White Witch, who makes it "always winter and never Christmas." The children are fortunate enough to meet Mr. and Mrs. Beaver, friendly creatures who are no allies of the White Witch. Like all animals in Narnia, the beavers can talk:

"Are you the Sons of Adam and the Daughters of Eve?" [Mr. Beaver] said.

"We're some of them," said Peter.

"S-s-s-sh!" said the Beaver, "not so loud please. We're not safe even here. . . ."

Here the Beaver's voice sank into silence and it gave one or two mysterious nods. Then signalling to the children to stand as close around it as they possibly could, so that their faces were actually tickled by its whiskers, it added in a low whisper—

"They say Aslan is on the move—perhaps has already landed."

And now a very curious thing happened. None of the children knew who Aslan was any more than you do; but the moment the Beaver had spoken these words everyone felt quite different. . . . At the name of Aslan each of the children felt something jump in his inside. Edmund felt a sensation of mysterious horror. Peter felt suddenly brave and adventurous. Susan felt as if some delicious smell or some delightful strain of music had just floated by her. And Lucy got the feeling you have when you wake up in the morning and realize that it is the beginning of the holidays or the beginning of summer.

—C. S. Lewis, *The Lion, The Witch and the Wardrobe* (New York: Collier Books, 1970), pp. 63-65. Permission granted by The C. S. Lewis Company Ltd., April 2010.

They say Aslan is on the move. The quiet rumor starting to rumble throughout the frozen land of Narnia is that the great lion Aslan, the true king of Narnia, is about to reclaim his kingdom and set things right. The world of Narnia is about to change. Aslan is on the move!

The Bible tells the story of how the God of this universe is *on the move.* In a dark and broken world, God is on the move to make all things new. The God of the Bible is not an absent God who stays away, nor a passive God who sits back and lets the world destroy itself. This God who *so loves the world* is actively present, entering into the mess and darkness of the world to bring new life.

All through the Bible we see God on the move, but this comes into clearest focus in the person of Jesus of Nazareth. On the first Easter morning, when the women came with arms full of spices and hearts empty of hope, they discovered that the stone had been rolled away. Staring into the empty tomb, the women, like the four children in the Narnia story, felt something inside them come alive. The world had changed. In the risen Jesus, God was on the move!

To be disciples of Jesus means that we are also on the move! Disciples *follow* Jesus. And where does Jesus lead us? *Into the world to join God's mission,* that's where. By the power of the Holy Spirit, we follow Jesus in all that we think, say, and do in order to be the presence of Christ in this lost and broken world that God so loves. You can't truly be a disciple of Jesus without caring about God's mission in the world.

This study is about mission. Chances are, most of us associate the word *mission* with a two-week trip to rebuild homes or a line item in the church budget or a person who brings the gospel to faraway places. All of these certainly are a part of God's mission, and are important to the life and work of the church. But mission encompasses so much more. Recently the word *missional* has been getting a lot of attention among Christians, followed by an avalanche of books and articles, all trying to get at the heart of what this word means.

Here's what I mean by *missional*: it is *the call to join in God's mission in the world to redeem the whole creation*. I want to challenge you to think about mission not as another program or activity at church or as "another thing" to add to your already busy life but as a *lifestyle*. Think of mission not just as something that happens "over there" but "right here" in your own community. Think of yourself as a *missionary*. It sounds kind of intimidating. But try not to let the word intimidate you. To think and live as a missionary means seeing *all of your life* as a way to be engaged with the mission of God in the world.

Seriously. *All* of life. Throwing in another load of laundry, changing dirty diapers, driving kids to soccer practice, preparing for a meeting, punching in for another shift, interacting with coworkers, getting to know your next-door neighbors, volunteering at the soup kitchen . . . all of it is the stuff of joining God's mission. Maybe you haven't thought about it this way. My hope is that this study will help you to change the way you see your own life, and that it will open your eyes to the way God is on the move in the everyday places you go and the people you meet.

So let's get started. *God is on the move.* Are you ready to be on the move with God? Are you ready for an adventure? There's nothing more satisfying to be a part of than this kingdom of God movement! "As the Father has sent me," says Jesus, "so I send you" (John 20:21).

Jesus is sending *you*.

God on the Move: The Missionary God of the Bible

The Biblical Drama of God's Mission

"For God so loved the world that he gave his only Son, so that everyone who believes in him may not perish but may have eternal life. Indeed, God did not send the Son into the world to condemn the world, but in order that the world might be saved through him."
—*John 3:16-17*

Imagine that you've stumbled upon the dusty old script of a play written by William Shakespeare, lost hundreds of years ago. No one else knows about the script you're now holding in your hands. As you begin to read, you notice that this play is written in six acts. You read through the first four acts in their entirety, but when you get to Act 5, you discover a problem. A big chunk of Act 5 is missing. After the first scene, there are no more. Oddly enough, Act 6, the final act, is intact.

Let's say you have some friends who happen to be actors, and they're intimately familiar with the works of Shakespeare. You share with them your remarkable discovery and the problem of the missing scenes of Act 5. You ask if they could reconstruct the missing part, based on their knowledge of Shakespeare.

A couple weeks later, after immersing themselves in the script, the actors perform the play for you. When they get to the missing scenes, they improvise. Brilliant! Their improvisation fits seamlessly with the four acts that came before and the final act that follows. It's as though none of the script had ever been missing.

How on earth did they manage that? By allowing their performance to be shaped by the first four acts and by the trajectory of the final act, the actors were able to get into character and move the plot along until it reached the author's intended conclusion.

Bible scholar Tom Wright offers this helpful analogy for reading, interpreting, and finding our own place in God's story. Wright suggests that the Bible is the drama of God's redemptive work in this world. It unfolds in five acts: creation (Act 1); the fall into sin (Act 2); Israel's story (Act 3); the story of Jesus Christ (Act 4); the story of God's people, the church (Act 5); and Christ's return, the grand conclusion we are still waiting for (Act 6).

At its heart, the biblical drama is about God and what God is doing in the world. We discover right away in the first three acts of this drama that God is a *missionary* God. God has not left us, even after the tragic second act when sin entered the picture and made a mess of things. Instead God moved onto the stage of human history. God made a covenant with Abraham and chose a people, Israel, to participate in God's mission to renew the whole creation.

The story comes to a shocking climax in Act 4, when God became human in the person of Jesus of Nazareth. In his life, death, and resurrection, Jesus fulfilled the mission of Israel, who failed to keep the covenant and be a light to the nations.

But the story doesn't end there. At the end of Act 4, Jesus enlisted a group of followers to be a part of his kingdom movement. He appeared to them as the risen One and breathed his Spirit on them. "As the Father has sent me," he said, "so I send you."

And that's where we come into the story—Act 5. But, like the players in the Shakespeare drama with missing scenes, we don't have a script in front of us. We have the final act, the book of Revelation, describing how God wins. We know how the story ends. So we're going to have to *improvise* our part, attentive to our own unique cultural situation. Our challenge is to stay consistent with the scenes that have gone before and the trajectory of how the story ends as we improvise in a new time and place. This is what missional living is all about: sticking with the past *and* following the Holy Spirit's lead as we face the fresh challenges of the present.

Over the next five weeks, we're going to spend some time absorbing this script into our bones and seeking the Spirit's leading as we explore what it means to do faithful missional improvisation!

Blessed to Be a Blessing:
The Story of Abraham and Israel

"I will make of you a great nation, and I will bless you,
and make your name great, so that you will be a blessing. . . .
In you all the families of the earth shall be blessed."
—*Genesis 12:2-3*

n 2008, Barack Obama was elected as the forty-fourth President of the United States, the first African American to serve in the nation's highest political office.

After this historic election, Richard Mouw, president of Fuller Theological Seminary, made this point: imagine that after being sworn into office, President Obama spent the next four years replaying how well he'd run his campaign and how deserving he was to fill this special office, but did nothing to carry out his new responsibilities. If that were to happen, even his most enthusiastic supporters wouldn't reelect him for a second term. That's because we elect the President to office *for a purpose*: with the privilege of being chosen comes great responsibility.

Act 2 of the biblical drama ends on a tragic note. After Act 1, when God spoke all creation into being and set the man and woman, made in his image, in the Garden, sin entered stage right—through the shrewd serpent and Adam and Eve's rebellion. Even after God purged the world of its wickedness with the flood and made a covenant with Noah and his family and all the animals of the earth, the human heart was still "prone to wander."

Genesis 10 tells of the world's nations emerging from the sons of Noah. The sad result of their multiplying and expansion is that humans fall into the same rebellious ways as their ancestors back in the Garden (Genesis 11). Driven by an all-consuming desire to build their own kingdom apart from God, they construct the tower of Babel. In response, God scatters humans across the face of the earth, mixing them up and confusing their language to prevent them from pursuing their puffed-up, grandiose projects.

Genesis 11 marks a climax in the advance of human sinfulness on the earth, but in Genesis 12 God's story takes a new direction with the opening scene of Act 3. God calls one man, Abram (later called Abraham), and makes an incredible promise: "I will make of you a great nation, and I will bless you, and make your name great, so that you will be a blessing. I will bless those who bless you, and the one who curses you I will curse; and in you all the families of the earth shall be blessed" (Genesis 12:2-3).

Abraham and his descendents have been elected by God. But the covenant God makes with them is not intended to allow them to bask in their own sense of being special. Abraham and his family, whose descendents would burgeon into the nation of Israel, were elected to be the instrument of God's mission, the spearhead of God's rescue operation for all people.

From the beginning, God called and blessed his people to be a channel of blessing to others. As they obey God, they demonstrate to the whole world what life under God's rule looks like. In them, the nations catch a glimpse of God's plan for all people.

We don't have to read much further to see that Israel doesn't always get this right. They fall into idolatry time and again, accommodating to the foreign cultures around them and forgetting their own story. And yet, even when Israel was unfaithful, God would remain faithful and unswervingly committed to his mission.

While Israel was in exile, the voices of prophets like Jeremiah, Ezekiel, and Isaiah reminded her of her place in God's story. For the first time the prophets spoke of a suffering servant who would fulfill Israel's mission and be a light to the nations. The Messiah, the Anointed One, would rise up from among them. Through this Messiah, Israel would be renewed and God's kingdom would finally be established over the whole earth, as he promised Abraham.

With this hope, the curtain falls at the end of Act 3.

Mission Accomplished: The Story of Jesus Christ

Jesus answered, "My kingdom is not from this world. If my kingdom were from this world, my followers would be fighting to keep me from being handed over to the Jews. But as it is, my kingdom is not from here."

—*John 18:36*

Here's a question: what is the central message of Jesus? Maybe you think it's "Love God and love others" or "I am the Way, the Truth, and the Life." Or "Trust in me and you will be saved." All of these are good answers, and some are direct quotes from the gospels. But none of them is the primary message Jesus preached.

Act 3 of the biblical drama ends with the prophetic promise of a Messiah who would rise from the "the stump of Jesse" to renew Israel and fulfill her mission to be God's channel of blessing for the whole world. Act 4 opens with the gospels, all telling the story of Jesus with their own unique flair. In the coming of Jesus, the story of God's salvation reaches a climax.

Mark's gospel opens this way: "The beginning of the good news of Jesus Christ, the Son of God." After Jesus is baptized by John in the Jordan River, Jesus begins his ministry in Galilee, "proclaiming the good news of God, and saying, 'The time is fulfilled, and the kingdom of God has come near; repent, and believe in the good news'" (Mark 1:14-15).

This is the central message of Jesus: *The kingdom of God has come near.* What did Jesus mean by "the kingdom of God" (also called "the kingdom of heaven" and "the reign of God")? This phrase may sound a little strange to those of us who live in a Western democracy. But those to whom Jesus was speaking were very familiar with his "kingdom" terminology.

You see, by the first century, there was widespread expectation among the Jews that God would do something dramatic to change the world. People had differing opinions about how God was going to act and what the Messiah would be like. But they all agreed that God would be faithful to the promises spoken by the prophets and bring them salvation.

So when Jesus announced that the kingdom of God was at hand, he was saying that God's long-anticipated time to save creation had arrived. The time had come for God's will to be done on earth as it is in heaven!

But Jesus not only *announced* that God's kingdom was near, he also *embodied* it. We see a glimpse of this in-breaking kingdom in Jesus' own person and actions—casting out demons, healing sick people, restoring sight to blind people, raising the dead, turning water into wine, calming the raging storm. All of these were signposts pointing to how things look when God's will is done on earth as it is in heaven—windows into the future of a renewed creation. Satan and his demons will have no power. Sickness and pain will be no more. Death will be destroyed. No trace of sin will deface God's new creation.

The climax of Jesus' mission is his death on a cross and his resurrection three days later, in which God defeated the powers of sin and death once and for all. By divine irony, the Roman cross—a symbol of shame and defeat in the first century—

became instrumental in overcoming the powers of darkness. The missionary God bursts out of the grave and moves, victorious, into the world. The world will never be the same.

How are we—God's people here and now—supposed to respond to the arrival of God's kingdom in Jesus? We are called to enter and receive this kingdom by *repentance* and *faith*. Repentance involves turning away from our old life of sin and toward Jesus, trusting him for a new life. Jesus calls those who have repented and believed to follow him. That means giving up our own way of life, receiving God's forgiveness through Christ, and following in his ways.

Jesus calls us to join him in his mission to be salt and light in the world. To follow Jesus is to become like him in all that we think, say, and do. It is to give him our full allegiance as King and our complete loyalty to his kingdom.

Be My Witnesses:
The Story of the Early Church

"But you will receive power when the Holy Spirit has come upon you; and you will be my witnesses in Jerusalem, in all Judea and Samaria, and to the ends of the earth."

—*Acts 1:8*

It was a wonderful moment. A group of us had travelled to Chiapas, Mexico, for a two-week cultural immersion experience, and on this particular Sunday we were worshiping with a local church. A man in his thirties stood up front with his wife and four young children. They had answered yes to Jesus' call to follow him. There they stood as a family, ready to be marked with the waters of baptism.

As the pastor poured handfuls of water on their heads, soaking their hair and clothes, I noticed the father's T-shirt. Advertising a soft drink company in the United States, it had the words *Mission Possible* on the back. It was the perfect phrase to describe this baptism unfolding in front of us! Because of what Christ has accomplished, our mission as disciples really *is* possible—and it's made possible by the Holy Spirit.

In yesterday's reading, we saw how God accomplished his mission in the life, death, and resurrection of Jesus. The cross and the empty tomb signal the arrival of the new age of God's kingdom. Act 5 of this biblical drama opens with the book of Acts, which tells the story of the spread of the kingdom through the mission of the early church.

As the book of Acts begins, the risen Jesus appears to his disciples over a period of forty days, during which there is much talk about the kingdom of God and the coming of the Spirit (1:3-5). The disciples ask Jesus the obvious question: "Lord, is this the time when you will restore the kingdom to Israel?" (1:6). Jesus answers, "It is not for you to know the times or periods that the Father has set by his own authority. But you will receive power when the Holy Spirit has come upon you; and you will be my witnesses in Jerusalem, in all Judea and Samaria, and to the ends of the earth" (1:7-8).

The kingdom of God has already broken into the present; however, it has not yet fully come. Jesus will ascend to the right hand of the Father, demonstrating his rule over all of creation, until he returns in the final day to bring his kingdom in fullness. But the disciples do not know when that day will come—only the Father knows. In the meantime, Jesus will send the Holy Spirit to clothe the disciples with power, drawing them into the life of the kingdom and empowering them to be witnesses of the kingdom to all nations. While Jesus was alive on earth, he mostly confined his ministry to Israel. Now, through his church, by the power of the Holy Spirit, Christ will multiply and extend his ministry "to the ends of the earth."

We see the movement of the Spirit begin in Jerusalem among the Jews and then move out into Samaria and the Judean countryside, pushing out further still to the ends of the earth to include even the Gentiles! While initially it was the apostles who were witnesses of the kingdom, soon others—"ordinary Christians"—were also empowered to witness.

With his death and resurrection, Jesus has already accomplished God's mission to save the world. As he burst from the tomb, God's kingdom had arrived. But it's not fully here. There's more to come. Since the birth of the church in Acts, we've been living "between" the times. While God's mission has been accomplished in Jesus, we've been baptized to *continue* Christ's mission. Better yet, we've been baptized to *demonstrate* what Jesus has already accomplished. We show the world what it looks like when Jesus is King; we invite all people to join us by living under his sovereign reign.

Think of it this way. An orchestra's job is not to compose music—that's already been done by the composer. Their job is to play the notes. Similarly, a football team's job is not to draft the playbook—that's already been done by the coach. Their job is simply to run the plays.

As God's people, our job is to play the notes on the musical score and run the plays in the playbook (with a little improvisation here and there)—to demonstrate God's new creation in Christ.

Act 5 of the divine drama continues today as we continue God's mission in our lives and in our world.

The Last Act: The New Heavens and New Earth

Then I saw a new heaven and a new earth; for the first heaven and the first earth had passed away. . . . And the one who was seated on the throne said, "See, I am making all things new."
—*Revelation 21:1, 5*

For her fourth birthday, my daughter Emma received a treasury of fairy tales. Her favorite was *Sleeping Beauty.* The first time I read her the story, Emma got scared and covered her eyes when Briar Rose fell asleep under the curse of the wicked fairy. She didn't want to read any further. I spoke some words of comfort and persuaded her to let me finish the story to its happy ending. The next time we read the story and came to the part where Briar Rose falls under the spell, I said to Emma, "Are you OK, honey?" To which she replied calmly, "Don't worry, Dad. I know how it ends!"

We are able to improvise as disciples here and now not only because we have the script of the prior four-and-a-half acts, but also because we know how God's story ends. We've been given the final act of the play. We know for certain that Christ is coming back. It's all going to be OK. We don't have to worry!

Throughout the biblical drama, God has given us previews of this final act: in the Old Testament we catch glimpses from prophets like Isaiah and Joel, and in the New Testament gospels the person, words, and actions of Jesus offer a window into God's kingdom. The last book of the Bible, however, presents a panoramic vision of God's future.

Revelation, which means *unveiling* in Greek, is one of the most fascinating and misunderstood books in the Bible. Many have treated this book as source for dire end-times charts that allow us to forecast the future. In fact, this type of Scripture is called "apocalyptic"—it is allegorical, not literal. Allegory uses images, symbols, and metaphors to convey a deeper spiritual meaning. And while Revelation points to the conclusion of God's story, it was written to give Jesus' disciples hope and courage in the present.

During a period when seven young churches in Asia Minor were undergoing persecution by the Roman Empire, God gives John, exiled on the island of Patmos, a vision to inspire them with hope and courage. It is as if the curtains of God's heavenly throne room are pulled back, and we catch a glimpse of the *truest reality*: no matter how dark the world seems, God is in control of human history.

With John, we catch a glimpse of the invisible spiritual battle that has been shaping our history. The outcome of this battle has already been determined: God wins! Satan and his dark forces are decisively defeated in the cross and resurrection of Jesus. They may wreak havoc for a time through worldly rulers and authorities and governments, but their fate has already been sealed. This was good news for the struggling Christians in first-century Asia Minor, and it is good news for us today.

The last chapters of Revelation show God's grand finale to this sprawling biblical drama. As promised, God will redeem this fallen creation. There will be a new heaven and a new earth entirely cleansed of sin and evil. The Holy City, the "new Jerusalem," will descend from heaven to earth. The new earth will be God's eternal dwelling place. God's kingdom, which started breaking in with Jesus' first coming, will come in fullness: "See, the home of God is among mortals. He will dwell with them as their God; they will be his peoples, and God himself will be with them; he will wipe every tear from their eyes. Death will be no more; mourning and crying and pain will be no more, for the first things have passed away" (Revelation 21:3-4).

Clearly God's intent is not to destroy the world, nor is it to whisk us up into a foggy realm called "heaven" to live for eternity as disembodied souls. Instead God is on the move to bring heaven to earth! The biblical view of salvation is not *escape* from earth; rather it is God's complete *restoration* of this world. We will spend eternity with God, in God's new creation, with new bodies.

So, like the first-century disciples to whom John wrote, we are actors in the biblical drama of God's story. Following the script that's gone before us, and immersing our imaginations in the last act of this remarkable play, we shape our lives to God's future. Jesus calls us to stand firm in the faith, to get into character and play our part with courage and innovation. "Behold, I am coming soon!" And we echo, "Amen! Come, Lord Jesus!"

Jesus is coming soon. Meanwhile, we echo the longing of John's own heart: "Amen! Come, Lord Jesus!"

Discussion Guide

Opening *(10 minutes)*

When you think of God as a "missionary God," what image or Bible story or personal experience comes to mind? Briefly share your thoughts without getting into any discussion or detail.

Then have someone read the following focus statement aloud:

> Mission is at the very heart of who God is and what God is up to in our world. Mission is not just a New Testament idea that begins with Jesus and the early church; rather, God has been on a mission since the first humans were sent east of Eden with their bags packed. Certainly God's mission reaches its fulfillment in Jesus and the New Testament church, but it has been going on long before. As we read the story of the Bible, let's pay attention to the way that mission is really the primary thrust of the whole biblical drama from beginning to end. And let's pay special attention to how mission is always first and foremost about God. Yes, we are invited to participate in God's mission. But it's always ultimately about who God is and how God is actively at work.

Bible Study *(20 minutes)*

Read as many of the following Bible passages as time permits. For each passage, ask: **How does this passage reveal the missionary heart of God?**

- Genesis 12:1-9
- Mark 1:14-28
- Acts 2:1-4, 14a, 22-39
- Revelation 21:1-8, 22-27

Activity Variation

Divide into groups or two or three, with each group taking one passage. Have each group summarize its passage and how it shows the missionary heart of God.

Alternate Approach

Jesus' parables were powerful and memorable ways for him to teach about God's kingdom breaking into the world. Have someone read aloud Luke's parable of the father and the two sons (Luke 15:11-32) while others act it out. Afterwards, talk about what you heard *and* saw. How did you experience this story differently seeing it acted out? What does this story reveal about the missionary heart of God?

Discussion *(20 minutes)*

As time permits, discuss some or all of the following questions, or use questions raised by group members.

1. Quickly review the six "acts" of the single drama of the Bible (Day 1). How does thinking this way about the Bible help you better understand it and its relevance for us today?

2. We often tend to associate *mission* with the New Testament and don't think of God as being "missionary" in the Old Testament. Why is this? What may make it difficult to see

God's missionary heart in the Old Testament? Where do you see God as "missionary" in the Old Testament?

3. Reread the paragraph (from Day 3) that begins, "But Jesus not only announced . . ." How does knowing that God's kingdom has already come in Jesus Christ affect you and the way you live day to day as a follower of Christ?

4. "We have the final act, the book of Revelation, describing how God wins. We know how the story ends. So we're going to have to *improvise* our part, attentive to our own unique cultural situation. Our challenge is to stay consistent with the scenes that have gone before and the trajectory of how the story ends as we improvise in a new time and place." (Day 1). What things must stay the same as we improvise for a new time and culture? What should change? In what ways does knowing the final act—how the story ends—make a difference as we improvise in the present?

5. What does the "final act" described in the book of Revelation (see Day 5) tell you about God? About our own future?

Closing *(5-10 minutes)*

Select one thought from the daily readings or one idea discussed in today's session that that will encourage or challenge you in your Christian living this week. Share it with the group.

As your closing prayer, sing or say together the words of the beloved hymn "Spirit of the Living God" (*Psalter Hymnal* 424).

Action Options

Being *missional* means moving beyond words into action. "As the Father has sent me," says Jesus, "so I send you" (John 20:21). While there are many ways to serve, you may want to consider the following action options for the group and for yourself:

Group: Brainstorm some ways your group could participate in God's mission by reaching out to others. For example, do you know of a shut-in in your church or community who could use a meal once a week? Or could the group volunteer to serve at a local food pantry or provide transportation for an elderly person to the store and doctor appointments? Group members will likely have other ideas appropriate to your group and local situation. Your deacons may also have ideas for how the group could serve.

Personal: Here are a couple of suggestions, but feel free to substitute your own ideas.

Option 1
If you feel the need to become more familiar with the whole dramatic script of the Bible, choose a plan that helps you read through the Bible in a year, or find some resources that help you better understand the larger story (such as *The True Story of the Whole World: Finding Your Place in the Biblical Drama*, Faith Alive, 2009, or online resources such as www.BibleGateway.com).

Option 2
Read Genesis 12:1-3 and 15:1-6, the story of how Abraham and Sarah were blessed by God to be a blessing to others. Practice being a channel of God's blessing this week. Look for opportunities to bless others through a spoken word, a listening ear, or an act of service.

A Church on the Move:
The Missionary People of God

Don't Go to Church; *Be* the Church!

But you are a chosen race, a royal priesthood, a holy nation, God's own people, in order that you may proclaim the mighty acts of him who called you out of darkness into his marvelous light. Once you were not a people, but now you are God's people. . . .
—*1 Peter 2:9-10*

Some time ago I was at a ministry conference. Seated at my table was a guy in his early twenties, powerfully built with colorful tattoos decorating his forearms. The words written in bold white letters on the front of his black T-shirt got my attention: DON'T GO TO CHURCH. I have to admit I was initially offended. *Who does he think he is, telling people not to go to church?* But when he excused himself and turned to walk away, I saw the words on the back of the T-shirt that completed the message: *BE* THE CHURCH.

Don't go to church; be the church.

When we think about the church, often the first thing that comes to mind is a building—the place we go on Sunday morning. As children, many of us learned this memorable rhyme, complete with hand motions: "Here's the church/ here's the steeple/ open the doors/ see all the people!" We distinguish between the church (the building, or a set of programs or activities, or worship services) and the people who attend. That attitude is also reflected in the way we talk about church: "Where do you go to church?" we say, or "I went to church last Sunday."

Not only do we tend to think of the church as *a place* where we go, but our consumer culture encourages us to view the church as a place to meet our needs. In this view, the church is a vendor of religious goods and services that delivers the spiritual product we want. And if we don't get what we want, we'll take our business elsewhere—maybe to the church down the street. In this scenario, the church may begin to pour its energy and resources into marketing and attracting customers and keeping those customers happy, as if it were a religious shopping mall, or like a religious country club that exists for the sake of its members: we pay our dues, and in return we expect membership perks.

This is not the picture of the church we see in the New Testament. God is a missionary God who seeks out people who are lost and broken. The church exists for the sake of joining God in mission, for the sake of other people. It is not a building or set of programs or organizational structures; it is the *people*. That young man's T-shirt had it exactly right: we don't *go* to church, we *are* the church!

The church is the missionary people of God *sent* to join in what God is doing in the world. "As the Father has sent me," Jesus said, "so I send you" (John 20:21).

What does it mean to be *sent*? It means we are called to live as a community under God's reign. We are called to demonstrate an alternative set of values from the rest of the world. We are sent to be a light to the nations and the salt of the earth, showing the world what it looks like when Jesus is King. In a nutshell, being sent means living *in* the world but *not of* the world.

Being sent also means that we are called to be on the move along with God. For too long we have hunkered down, circled our wagons, and waited for others to come to us. We set up in a building and offer excellent worship services and relevant programs, expecting that those outside the church will be attracted and come to us. But being sent requires us to *go into the world* and meet others where they are *on their own turf.*

Following Jesus, we practice an *incarnational* ministry. Jesus is God made human, he moved into the neighborhood (John 1:18, *The Message*). Like him we incarnate the good news; we move into the neighborhood to bear witness to God's kingdom erupting all around us.

There is no greater adventure than getting swept up into this kingdom movement that is turning the world upside down and right side up! So let's not *go* to church; let's *be* the church—a Christ-centered, Spirit-filled people who are on the move and passionately living out our faith every day in this lost and broken world that God so loves!

The Church as a Sign of the Kingdom

Although I am the very least of all the saints, this grace was given to me to bring to the Gentiles the news of the boundless riches of Christ, and to make everyone see what is the plan of the mystery hidden for ages in God who created all things; so that through the church the wisdom of God in its rich variety might now be made known to the rulers and authorities in the heavenly places.
—Ephesians 3:8-10

Every year around September my family has a tradition of going apple-picking. We drive about twenty miles south on back roads, rolling hills, and curves to a rural area. Since you can't see the orchard from the road, we're all on the lookout for the large painted sign that announces "Crane Apple Orchards."

Of course, the Crane's sign is not the orchard itself. The sign simply identifies the location and directs us to the actual orchard. Like any good sign, it marks and represents the reality to which it points. It gets our attention and directs us to the real thing beyond itself.

The church, God's missionary people, is a *sign* too. It's a sign of God's kingdom. God's kingdom is not the same thing as the church. And yet the church is inseparable from God's kingdom. The church is a sign of that kingdom in the sense that it directs people's attention to God's gracious presence and activity in the world.

In Acts 1:8, Jesus declares to his disciples "You are my witnesses." One of the ancient understandings of *witness* was of a herald who ran out ahead into the villages and towns to announce that a new king had been enthroned. This is our task as witnesses of God's kingdom. As a community and as individuals we go into the world—to our families and neighborhoods, main streets and back alleys, shopping malls and slums, workplaces and schools—and announce: "There is a new King. His name is Jesus. Receive his forgiveness; turn from your old life and follow him."

Of course being a witness of Jesus is not always a popular thing to be. It's more likely to invite resistance and conflict. After all, when we announce that a new king has been enthroned, the established powers and authorities aren't going to be pleased. The status quo gets disrupted, and that means the world is changing. The Greek word for *witness* is *martyria,* and it's true that the earliest witnesses of Christ were martyrs for their allegiance to this new king and his kingdom.

By God's grace, most of the people reading this book will likely never be physically persecuted or killed for their faith (although this is a reality today for some of our Christian brothers and sisters around the world). But to follow Jesus does mean that we die to our old way of life and to our selfish agendas and projects. We deny ourselves, take up our crosses, and follow our Lord. In *The Cost of Discipleship,* Dietrich Bonhoeffer issues this sobering call for Christians of every time and place: "When Christ calls a man, he bids him come and die."

We are all called to live a life of martyrdom. We die to sin and ourselves in order to be raised to new life in Christ. We surrender ourselves to the way of Jesus. This is what it means to be a witness. And this new life in Jesus is the only life worth living *and* dying for!

The Church as a Foretaste of the Kingdom

He is the head of the body, the church. . . . For in him all the
fullness of God was pleased to dwell, and through him God was
pleased to reconcile to himself all things, whether on earth or in
heaven, by making peace through the blood of his cross.
—*Colossians 1:18-20*

Whenever my wife and I get the opportunity to go see a movie in the theater (a rare occasion since we've become parents), I try to arrive early to catch the previews. Some people find previews annoying—they just want to get on to the main feature. Not me. I love previews. I enjoy getting a taste of the new movies that are coming out soon.

In yesterday's reading, we saw how the church is a *sign* of God's kingdom. But it is also a *foretaste* of God's kingdom. The church not only points beyond itself to God's presence and activity in the world, it also *embodies* it! In our life together as the church, we are a *preview* of what is to come—a glimpse here and now of what life looks like when God rules, and of the bright future God intends for all of creation.

Of course this doesn't mean that we are without sin. Sixteenth-century reformer Martin Luther wrote that Christians are simultaneously saints and sinners. In baptism, he said, our old self is put to death and our new self rises with Christ—but we learn very soon that the old self is a mighty good swimmer! And yet, as we follow in the way of Christ and are transformed into the very image of Jesus by the power of the Holy Spirit, there should be something different about the way we live that gets the world's attention.

This way of life is marked by love instead of hatred, forgiveness instead of bitterness, kindness instead of cruelty, mercy instead of vengeance, peace and justice instead of violence and indifference. It is the way marked by the fruits of the Holy Spirit. It turns the world's values and priorities upside-down.

One Sunday morning in my first parish, a rural congregation in the Midwest, we were getting ready to celebrate communion together. Ten years earlier, two women in the congregation, Susan and Janice, had participated in an ugly falling-out. Ever since, they'd had nothing to do with each other. That morning I preached a sermon on being reconciled to each other. I said that communion is a sign of our unity. I told the congregation how important it is for us to be reconciled to each other before we come to this meal. Afterward we spent a few minutes passing Christ's peace with one another.

Amidst all the commotion, I looked up and noticed Susan and Janice awkwardly looking at one another from across the aisle. At first, neither of them moved a muscle. Then Susan stepped sideways down the pew to the center aisle. She hesitated and then walked over to where Janice was standing. They stood there face to face, neither saying a word. Then Susan's face relaxed. Her eyes teared as she reached out and hugged Janice. She whispered, "I'm sorry. Will you forgive me?" Janice returned her embrace and asked for forgiveness also.

The moment didn't last long. The "Hallelujah" chorus didn't break out in the sanctuary, nor did angels descend from the ceiling rafters. In fact, I'm guessing most people missed the whole thing. But I saw it. Something truly "gospel" happened. I witnessed a foretaste of God's kingdom as these two women chose forgiveness over holding on to a long-nursed grudge.

Recent studies show that when many people outside the church look in, they don't see Jesus—that is, they don't see a preview of God's kingdom. In fact, what they see in the church often points them *away* from Jesus. This is a travesty. It is critical to our witness that we truly strive, by the power of the Holy Spirit, to show the world God's future for all of creation. Like John the Baptist, we're called to point people to the true Savior and King.

The Church as an Instrument of the Kingdom

So we are ambassadors for Christ, since God is making his appeal through us; we entreat you on behalf of Christ, be reconciled to God.
—*2 Corinthians 5:20*

We've talked about how God's missionary people are both a *sign* and a *foretaste* of God's kingdom. Today we'll focus on one more important aspect of the church's calling in relation to God's kingdom—the church is God's primary *instrument* of his rescue operation to renew all of creation. Not only is the church called to point beyond itself and offer a preview of God's future, but *through* the church's witness God intends to bring about the renewal of the whole world.

Paul writes, "All this is from God, who reconciled us to himself through Christ, and has given us the ministry of reconciliation; that is, in Christ God was reconciling the world to himself, not counting their trespasses against them, and entrusting the message of reconciliation to us. So we are ambassadors for Christ, since God is making his appeal through us" (2 Corinthians 5:18-20).

We are Christ's ambassadors, and he is doing his work of reconciliation through us. Not only does God bring reconciliation within the church, among God's people, God intends to bring reconciliation to all parts of this world through the church—not only human beings, societies, and nations, but the *whole creation.* "We know that the whole creation has been groaning in labor pains until now" says Paul (Romans 8:22).

The church is the instrument God chooses to bring about the work of redemption in the world. God has not given up on the church! God has entrusted the message of reconciliation to us—God's people. God calls us to be Christ's presence in this lost and broken world God loves.

Howard and his wife, Judy, owned a number of homes in their community and rented them to tenants. One day Mary, a single mom, moved to town with her five children. They were looking to make a fresh start after escaping from an abusive boyfriend. They didn't have much money. Howard worked with Mary so that she could rent one of his houses for minimal cost.

Howard saw his work as a landlord as a *ministry.* It was his way of being an ambassador of Christ. So he developed relationships with his tenants and took the time to get to know them. He and Judy took a special interest in Mary and her kids. They reached out by stocking her pantry with food and providing extra clothes for the kids. They made a special effort to check in on Mary several times a week.

But Howard and Judy didn't stop there. Judy helped Mary write a résumé and taught her some basic finance skills and how to put together a budget. Howard, a member of city council, helped Mary get a custodial job at the local hospital. Howard and Judy noticed that Mary was self-conscious about her teeth, so she never smiled. They offered to pay for her to have some dental work done. Mary was overwhelmed with their kindness—no one had ever treated her with such generosity and loving concern. She accepted their offer, and almost immediately they could see how much the dental work boosted her self-confidence.

Eventually Howard and Judy invited Mary and her children to join their church family, and Mary gave her life to Jesus. One of my favorite memories as a pastor is of the Sunday we baptized Mary and her five children. I can still see the way Mary smiled that day as I poured water on her head and on all her children—the biggest, most radiant smile, without a hint of shame. When I said to the congregation, "Welcome the newest members of God's family!" the whole place erupted with applause.

Howard and Judy and their congregation were ordinary Christians and extraordinary instruments of God's kingdom in their small Midwest town. Of course, the power to bring healing and reconciliation to Mary and her family didn't reside in them—it was the power of Christ working through them. They were simply Christ's ambassadors.

DAY 5

Moving from Attractional to Incarnational

The Word became flesh and blood,
and moved into the neighborhood.

—*John 1:14*, The Message

Over twenty years ago the movie *Field of Dreams* was released. It tells the story of a farmer named Ray Kinsella. One day Ray is walking through his cornfield, when out of the blue a mysterious voice whispers, "If you build it, they will come." *It* turns out to be a baseball field smack in the middle of his lush, green cornfield.

For a long time now, the church has operated with an "If we build it, they will come" mentality. If we find a strategic location, hire dynamic staff, provide excellent worship services, and offer an impressive menu of programs and activities, we think, people will come out in droves and our membership will soar. Unfortunately this "attractional" model of ministry more often draws Christians from other churches than it draws people who are disconnected from God.

Don't get me wrong. There's something to be said about God's people being a "light on a hill" and drawing the world's attention because of the way we are set apart as Christ's followers. But we've already noted that God's missionary heart is on the move. God doesn't sit back and wait for us to come to him—our sinful condition makes it impossible for us to find our way back to God, even if we tried. No, in his grace and radical love, God makes the first move. God seeks *us* out! God has already come to us most decisively and powerfully in the incarnation—taking on human form in the person of Jesus of Nazareth. "The Word became flesh and blood," the gospel writer John writes, "and moved into the neighborhood."

As God's missionary people, then, Christ summons us to follow him into the world and meet people where they are. It is not sufficient for the church to simply huddle back and hope to attract those who are suffering, lost, confused, and searching.

An *incarnational* model of ministry places the highest value on building relationships and inviting others to join us in the spiritual journey instead of simply putting on programs. Although programs are usually necessary to do ministry, programs must always serve relationships, not the other way around.

An incarnational model of ministry sees the whole community as a mission field and seeks to get to know people in the community to better understand their deepest needs, fears, hopes, and concerns. It is just as concerned, if not more, about what Leonard Sweet has called "sending capacity" as it is with "seating capacity." It is to be just as concerned about *releasing God's people into the community* as it is with getting the community into the church building.

Here's one of my favorite stories about incarnational ministry.

Esther and Leila are two women in their mid-seventies. Esther's great-grandson got into trouble with the law and was incarcerated in the county prison sixty miles away. Esther decided to visit him one day and bring some fresh-baked cookies. She invited Leila to ride along with her. When they

47

got there, they were amazed to discover how many young men were in the prison, and how few of them had any visitors.

The following week they asked the women in their women's group to bake a few dozen cookies. They placed them on plates, wrapped them with foil, and attached a little card that said "Jesus loves you!" Esther and Leila returned to the prison and delivered cookies to every single one of the inmates. They took the time to learn the names of each young man and to learn a little of his story. They promised to pray for each of them. One young man, Danny, was particularly touched by their kindness. When Esther and Leila gave him the plate of cookies, he said, "How'd you know it was my birthday today? You're the only person who remembered!"

Esther and Leila continued to visit the prison every other week, bringing other friends with them and building relationships with these young men. When they started a Bible study, around a dozen young men showed up and kept coming back.

Esther and Leila's prison ministry reminds me of Jesus' words when he stood up in the temple to announce Isaiah's prophetic words: "The Spirit of the Lord is upon me, because he has anointed me to bring good news to the poor. He has sent me to proclaim release to the captives and recovery of sight to the blind, to let the oppressed go free, to proclaim the year of the Lord's favor" (Luke 4:18-19).

The Spirit of the Lord was upon Esther and Leila to proclaim the good news to a group of young men in a county prison. What a wonderful example of incarnational ministry—daring to venture out and be the presence of Christ to people wherever they are!

Discussion Guide

Opening *(10 minutes)*

Begin by going around the group and sharing about your experience with the church. Did you grow up in the church or become part of it later in life? Has your experience generally been positive or negative?

Then have someone read the following focus statement aloud:

> The primary reason the church exists is not for itself alone but to participate in God's mission in and for the world. How do we participate in God's mission? In our readings this week we explored three aspects of the church's identity and vocation: as a *sign*, a *foretaste*, and an *instrument* of God's kingdom. The church is not ultimately a building or set of programs; it is God's covenant people sent into the world, blessed in order to be a blessing. As we die to our old lives and are united to Jesus by the power of the Holy Spirit, God's blessing flows through us and makes a difference in the world.

Bible Study *(15 minutes)*

Read Acts 2:42-47 and then answer these questions:

- What key practices did the early Christians devote themselves to in this passage? How do we continue to devote ourselves to these things today?
- Identify the values embraced by the fellowship of believers. How do they treat one another? How do these values compare to the values and customs of our North American culture?
- Acts 2:47 states: "Day by day the Lord added to their number those who were being saved." How do the words "The Lord added to their number" reflect the idea of a "missional" God?

Discussion *(20 minutes)*

As time permits, discuss some or all of the following questions, or use questions raised by group members.

1. Discuss the difference between the view of the church as "a club that exists for its members" and as "a covenant community that exists for God's mission in the world." If you were to locate your church on this spectrum between "a club for insiders" on one side and "engaging God's mission to embrace others" on the other side, where would your church land right now?

2. According to the reading for Day 2, the church is a sign of God's kingdom but it is not identical with God's kingdom. Why is this distinction important?

3. How is your congregation faithfully being a foretaste of God's kingdom? In other words, in what ways is your church offering a preview of God's future for the whole world? Does a specific story—such at the one about Susan and Janice in the reading for Day 3—come to mind?

4. Where do you see your church being "an instrument of God's kingdom" (Day 4), making a difference in your community

and the world? Is there a ministry you'd like to see your church start or a way your church could more effectively be God's instrument in your specific area?

5. Imagine having a conversation with someone who explains, "I'm a very spiritual person but I'm not really into organized religion. I believe in Jesus, but I don't really like the church." How would you respond?

Alternate Approach

Rather than use the five discussion questions above, walk back through each daily reading with the group, having group members raise their own questions and comments about the readings.

Closing (5-10 minutes)

Have a group member read the following statement about the church:

There is nothing like the local church when it is working right. Its beauty is indescribable. Its power is breathtaking. Its potential is unlimited. It comforts the grieving and heals the broken in the context of community. It builds bridges to seekers and offers truth to the confused. It provides resources for those in need and opens its arms to the forgotten, the downtrodden, the disillusioned. It breaks the chains of addictions, frees the oppressed, and offers belonging to the marginalized in this world. Whatever the capacity for human suffering, the church has a greater capacity for healing and wholeness.

—Bill Hybels, *Courageous Leadership* (Grand Rapids: Zondervan, 2002), p. 23.

Then spend some time in prayer. Allow time for group members to share personal joys and concerns. Here are some additional suggestions:

- Give thanks for the way God's kingdom is breaking in among us, and for the ways in which our churches strive to be faithful witnesses to God's kingdom.
- Pray for God's Spirit to overcome the barriers that may be preventing our churches from embracing a more incarnational model of ministry.
- Pray for the witness of the church around the world as a way of being mindful of how large and diverse the body of Christ is. Pray especially for brothers and sisters in other places who endure persecution and violence for their courageous witness.

Action Options

Group: If your church has a mission statement, bring it to the group. Discuss whether the mission statement is *attractional* or *missional/incarnational*. Does it put the focus on God (Father, Son, and Holy Spirit) or on human effort? If you think it's needed, take a shot at shot at revising your church's mission statement to make it more missional. If your church doesn't have a mission statement, try writing one.

Personal: In the coming week, move out of your comfort zone to interact with someone who is in need or is different from you or who seems disconnected from God. Maybe this means walking across the room to have a conversation with a coworker. Or maybe it means making a special effort to interact with a neighbor who doesn't know Christ. Maybe God is stirring enough courage in your heart to go and serve somewhere you don't usually go (the local homeless shelter, Boys and Girls Club, a soup kitchen). Or perhaps God is calling you to develop a relationship with someone in a place you *do* usually go (the waitress at your favorite restaurant, a parent whose child plays on your child's soccer team, a familiar face across the shop floor). The point is to be intentional about going out and meeting people where they are, on their turf.

Cultivating a Missional Imagination

A New Way of Seeing

*From now on, therefore, we regard no one from a human point of
view; even though we once knew Christ from a human point of view,
we know him no longer in that way. So if anyone is in Christ,
there is a new creation: everything old has passed away;
see, everything has become new!*
—2 Corinthians 5:16-17

The great Michelangelo was once seen transporting a huge
rock through the busy streets of Florence. The citizens,
who wondered why he would go to so much effort for
something so ordinary and unattractive, asked, "Why are you
pushing that mighty rock, Michelangelo?" His response was
simple: "Because there's a person inside longing to get out!"
From this huge, unattractive rock, Michelangelo would sculpt
his masterpiece, the "David."

Imagination has to do with our way of seeing. It determines
the way we see and interpret reality. A *missional imagination,*
then, describes *our capacity to see God's presence and activity
among us.* Even more, a missional imagination is *the capacity*

to see God's future bursting forth in the most ordinary places. Like Michelangelo, a missional imagination looks at a rock and sees something more than just a rock. It sees the masterpiece within—the possibilities of beauty, hope, justice.

A missional imagination does not take the world at face value. It knows that more is going on than meets the eye. There's a great line in U2's hit song "Moment of Surrender" that talks about "vision over visibility." A missional imagination sees things through the eyes of faith—it sees a vision for what God intends over the visibility of a world that's not the way it's supposed to be. When we turn on the news or pick up a newspaper and are inundated with stories of tragedy, pain, and violence, a missional imagination sees beyond appearances to the truth that God is on the move, bringing about new creation.

C.S. Lewis once talked about how his imagination needed to be baptized. Like the rest of us, our imagination is fallen because of sin. Held captive, it needs to be set free. Paul writes in Romans, "Do not be conformed to this world, but be transformed by the renewing of your minds." In Christ, by the power of the Holy Spirit, God has redeemed our imaginations and set them free. We are given the gift of an imagination that is capable of recognizing God's presence and activity among us, of seeing what the world looks like when Christ is King.

While a missional imagination is a gift of God's grace received by faith, we have a part to play. Our job is to cultivate this missional imagination so that it grows and develops. I like this organic word *cultivate*—maybe because I grew up in the country, my own backyard hedged in by a beautiful sea of corn and beans. Good farmers know they can't make growth happen. Their job is to faithfully cultivate the condition of the soil so that the miracle of growth can take place. The same is true for us if we are to develop robust missional imaginations. Although God's Spirit is the one who renews our minds, our responsibility is to cultivate the conditions in our lives so that, rather than being conformed to the ways of the world, our baptized imaginations will flourish and see the reality of God's kingdom.

God has always used ordinary people as agents of his extra-ordinary purposes. Cultivating a missional imagination is learning to see the masterpiece hidden in the rock. It is learning to see what God is doing in our ordinary lives and envisioning a future that is different from the present arrangement.

This week's readings will explore some key practices that will help you cultivate the conditions in your own life for God to renew and shape your imagination for mission. We'll explore how worship is the primary context in which the missional imagination gets shaped, the central role of reading the Bible and finding ourselves in God's story, developing a deeper prayer life, and other practices that make room for God's trans-formational work in our lives.

Worship: Where the Missional Imagination Gets Shaped

*Worship the L*ORD *in holy splendor;*
tremble before him, all the earth.

—Psalm 96:9

He was a mesmerizing speaker. Genuine, passionate, with a great sense of humor that made him endearing. He was speaking to a large crowd of pastors and lay leaders about what it means to have a missional approach to ministry. I was tracking right along with him (saying some *Amen*s under my breath) until he came to the part about worship. "Maybe Christians would be acting more missionally," he asserted, "if they decided one Sunday morning to cancel worship and go out and serve their community instead! Then we'd really show the world what it means to be the church!" All around me, heads nodded agreement.

The impulse to go into our community and neighborhoods and serve in Jesus' name is certainly right. But to suggest that we are acting in a more missional way when we are out of the sanctuary and serving in the streets, or that worship itself is not all that important, is to drastically misunderstand the significance of worship for disciples. While it's certainly easy for our worship to become about us (instead of God), or for a life of discipleship to get reduced to an hour-a-week experience, the fact remains that *worship is essential to cultivating a missional imagination.* In fact, I suggest that worshiping together with God's missionary people is the primary context that shapes the missional imagination!

First, worship is *an end in itself.* We worship first and foremost because God has commanded us to worship him alone. God is worthy of our praise. In a world teeming with idols at every turn, all working to seduce us and win our loyalty, there may not be a single more missional act than to worship God alone! We are not our own but belong to God in Christ Jesus.

Second, worship is *a means to an end* (but only after we recognize it first as an end in itself). Worship shapes us into a missional people. Once someone asked the late Robert Webber, who spent his life studying and thinking about worship, "In a single sentence, what *is* worship?" He answered: "Worship *does* God's story."

This interesting response suggests that worship—the liturgy, music, prayers, Scripture, preaching, and sacraments—tells the story of God's biblical drama. Our job as worshipers is to enact that story together.

How do we enact God's story in worship?

- First, *we remember God's faithfulness in the past.* We remember who God is, what God has already accomplished on our behalf in Jesus, and, consequently, who we are and why we are here.
- Second, *we become attentive to God's presence and activity in the present.* Every worship service is a celebration of resurrection— the living God (Father, Son, and Holy Spirit) is active among us even now. And by the power of the Holy Spirit, we are united with Jesus and share in the very life of God.
- Third, *worship anticipates the future.* It offers a preview of God's future for us and all creation. In worship, God's future

comes to meet us in the present. We get to see how the story ends! And it is good news: God will set all things right and make all things new.

Enacting God's story in worship glorifies God and also shapes us into the image of Jesus, into a missional people. We need to stop evaluating the quality of our worship based on questions such as "How did it make me feel?" or "What did I get out of that today?" or "Wow, I really liked that song." Faithful worship is best measured by questions like, "Are we being transformed more and more into the image of Jesus?" and "Are we ready to join God's mission in the world out of gratitude for who God is and what God has accomplished for us in Christ?"

So let's not think of worship as an option or as an inconvenience that keeps us from getting out there in the world to live missional lives. We can't live without it! We are shaped into a missional people by the stories we tell as we enact God's story together in worship.

The movement of a missional people is circular—*from* worship we are sent to engage in God's mission in the world, and *to* worship we return to declare God's glory and bring with us those whom we've embraced with the good news of the gospel.

Finding Ourselves in the Story: Reading the Bible Missionally

This is the story of how it all started,
of Heaven and Earth when they were created.
                                        —*Genesis 2:4*, The Message

I n *The Tale of Despereaux*, Kate DeCamillo tells the story of a small mouse with big ears named Despereaux Tilling. From the moment he was born, he didn't fit in with the rest of the mouse community. Instead of scurrying around doing typical "mouse things," Despereaux acquired a love for music and reading books. His favorite tales were of valiant knights who rescued a beautiful princess in distress. More than anything, Despereaux wanted to be one of these brave knights.

One day, Despereaux wanders into the dining hall of the king and sees the beautiful Princess Pea. It is love at first sight! When the mouse community learns that Despereaux has done the forbidden—that is, interacted with a human being—he is banished to the lower realm of the dungeon where rats lurk in the shadows.

Overcome with fear, Desperaux is led down the spiraling staircase. But a voice in his head tells him he must be brave. For the Princess, he must face the darkness with courage. Despereaux takes a deep breath, stands up straight, peers into the darkness, and speaks aloud the best words he knows. *Once upon a time there was a brave knight . . .* his quivering little voice calls out.

And as he speaks this story into the darkness, something wonderful happens. His pounding heart is filled with fresh courage. He finds himself *in* the story. *He* is the brave knight. This larger story shapes his imagination and changes his perspective. He starts acting like a brave knight instead of a frightened mouse.

Something similar happens when we read the Bible faithfully. The drama of God's mission provides us with a larger story that shapes our imagination and gives us a coherent vision of reality. As we saw in Day 1, we are characters in this story! In Act 5 of the drama, we enter the story to play our part as God's missionary people in this time and place.

Many of us have been taught to read the Bible as nothing more than an instruction book or an encyclopedia of information. Even worse, throughout history some horrible things have been done on the basis of *misreading* the Bible. As Harper Lee points out in her classic novel *To Kill a Mockingbird*, "sometimes the Bible in the hand of one man is worse than a whiskey bottle in the hand of another." Sad but true.

To read the Bible from a missional perspective is to read it not simply for information or to validate our own ideas, but for *spiritual transformation*. It is to recognize that the Bible, even with all its various parts, makes up a larger narrative about how God is on the move in human history. The Bible is the primary story that changes and shapes us, but it can only change and shape us if we enter the story. The Bible reads us just as much as we read it. Just like Despereaux, it makes something of us more than we make something of it.

How do we enter the story? By taking the Bible on its own terms. By fitting our experiences into the strange new world of the Bible rather than trying make the Bible relevant to our lives. When we encounter the morally flawed characters in the Bible, we see ourselves in them.

We read humbly, allowing ourselves to be swept into the story. And we read expectantly, believing that the Bible is a living Word that speaks afresh to us in our specific situation by the power of the Holy Spirit.

God wants to address us personally through the Bible. The question Jesus posed to his disciples two thousand years ago—and ever since—is this: *Do you have eyes to see and ears to hear?*

The Revolutionary Act of Prayer

For you did not receive a spirit of slavery to fall back into fear,
but you have received a spirit of adoption. When we cry,
"Abba! Father!" it is the very Spirit bearing witness with
our spirit that we are children of God. . . .

—Romans 8:15-16

" I guess there's nothing left to do but pray." It's funny how often, in our busy and self-reliant culture, we view prayer as a sort of "Hail Mary" pass for when all else fails and we don't know what to do next.

For Jesus and for the New Testament church, prayer was not a last resort. It was the *first* resort. Prayer was the primary activity around which everything else pivoted and from which all else flowed. It was the most potent ammunition against the principalities and powers of darkness. For Jesus and for the early church, prayer was the primary way to get in on God's mission in the world.

In Luke chapter 11, Jesus' disciples come and say, "Lord, teach us to pray as John taught his disciples." So Jesus teaches them a short, powerful prayer that is really a summary of his ministry—a prayer for God's future kingdom to break into the present. This is the prayer that we have come to know as "the Lord's Prayer" (see also Matthew 6:7-18).

The ancient liturgies still used in some denominations introduce the Lord's Prayer with the words, *Now, as our Savior Jesus Christ has taught us, we are bold to say* . . .

We *are* bold to pray this prayer. Stop for a minute and think about what we're really asking of God: "*Thy* will be done, *thy* kingdom come!" We are asking God to do not what we want but what *God* wants! It takes guts to pray this revolutionary prayer. "To speak those words," writes Fredrick Buechner, "is to invite the tiger out of the cage, to unleash a power that makes atomic power look like a warm breeze."

By the mystery of God's will, God unleashes the surging power of the Holy Spirit through our prayers. Our prayers have a role in shaping the future. I can't begin to explain to you how this mystery works, but it's something like this: the Holy Spirit choreographs our prayers—gives us the impulse to pray and shapes those prayers so as to bring about what God desires in the world.

So we don't have to know how to pray perfectly before we pray. Paul reassures us that the Holy Spirit intercedes for us, takes our sighs and groans and imperfect prayers and transforms them into prayers that reach the Father's ear and are according to God's will. The Lord's Prayer is so helpful because it gives us the words to speak, especially when we're not sure how to pray or what words to use. Of course it's not the *only* prayer or even *kind* of prayer we can pray. The Bible offers examples of many kinds of prayer. (For an explanation of various kinds of prayer, see Richard Foster's book *Prayer: Finding the Heart's True Home.*) And all prayer, no matter what kind, bends us toward God and opens us up to receive the Spirit's power.

Prayer unleashes God's power in the world. But perhaps the best thing about prayer is the way the power of the Holy Spirit is unleashed in *us.* "Prayers are not tools for getting or doing, but being and becoming," says Eugene Peterson. When we learn to pray, God changes us, transforms us more and more into disciples who are impassioned to join God in mission. God bends our wants and desires away from ourselves and toward his own missionary heart.

In this way, God uses us to become the answers to our prayers. As we practice praying the Lord's Prayer boldly, we find ourselves being transformed by the Holy Spirit to *live boldly* as disciples of Jesus—those who forgive and love recklessly and bear witness to the unleashing of a kingdom that is turning the world upside down. We are empowered to go out and feed poor people, visit those who are in prison, care for those who are orphaned and widowed, set captive people free, and declare the year of the Lord's favor.

This is the call of discipleship: to be changed by God so that, through us, God changes the world into which we've been sent.

Practice, Practice, Practice!

*Train yourself in godliness, for, while physical training is of some
value, godliness is valuable in every way, holding promise
for both the present life and the life to come.*
—1 Timothy 4:7-8

A couple of summers ago I finally did something I've
wanted to do for a very long time. I bought a road bike. I
decided on a Specialized Alliez—a sleek silver aluminum
frame with black and silver components. It's an entry-level
bike, but I got all the bells and whistles: clip-in peddles, a seat
designed for agility and comfort, two water bottle holders, and
a little computer that has more functions than I'll ever know
what to do with.

I knew that if I was going to see myself as a serious cyclist, I
needed to get all the right gear—gloves, helmet, a jersey, and
those padded bike shorts that I'm still embarrassed to wear in
public. I also devoured books and magazines on cycling. I even
bought Lance Armstrong's training manual. This was serious
business. I wasn't playing around.

I read up on cycling. I tried on all the gear and even wore it around the house. But the bike just sat in the garage.

For two weeks. It just sat there.

My imagination was *beginning* to be shaped as a cyclist by reading books and magazines and getting the right gear. But if I were truly going to be transformed into a cyclist, I needed to get on the bike and start riding. Beyond just knowing *about* my bike, I needed to practice actually riding it!

The same thing is true of being a disciple of Jesus. We can buy all the right accessories and read all the right books and magazines. We can have the best intentions. But if we're serious about developing a missional imagination and getting in on what God is doing in the world, we have to practice actually following Jesus. Living a missional life doesn't just happen—it takes practice, practice, practice!

That's why *spiritual disciplines* are so important. They help us practice becoming like Jesus in all we think, say, and do.

John Ortberg defines a spiritual discipline as "any activity that can help me gain power to live life as Jesus taught and modeled it." He goes on to make a helpful distinction between *trying* versus *training*. So many Christians think that the life of discipleship is about trying harder, mustering up more willpower. But it's not a matter of trying harder. It's a matter of *training* to be like Jesus every day, by the power of the Holy Spirit.

In our next session we're going to focus on missional improvisation. But before we can improvise well as disciples who follow Jesus in mission, it's necessary to train wisely so our imaginations can see the world from a missional point of view. That means putting ourselves in a place where God's grace can transform us from the inside out.

Jazz music is celebrated for its improvisation. But we'd be crazy to think that the all-time greats like Louis Armstrong, Mary Lou Williams, and Duke Ellington just picked up a trumpet one day or sat down at the piano and started improvising without ever practicing a musical scale or learning to train their ear. They're able to improvise so effectively *because of* all of the hours and years of training they put in. The same is true of the quarterback scrambling out of the pocket or the surgeon struggling to stop a bleed.

So it is with participating in God's mission. We need to cultivate a missional imagination by training wisely. We've explored some key spiritual disciplines in the daily readings this week: worship, reading the Bible, and prayer. These are the pillars of a life of training in discipleship. But there are more spiritual disciplines that can help us—disciplines like confession, fasting, solitude, submission, service, and celebration. (For a full list, see Richard Foster's *Celebration of Discipline*.)

The point is that missional improvisation takes practice. It's about cultivating an imagination that's shaped by God's story and not the dizzying array of competing stories in our culture. It's about practicing key disciplines that put us in a place for God's grace to change us.

It's about getting on the bike and actually *riding*!

Discussion Guide

Opening *(10 minutes)*

Option 1
Glance back through the five readings and pick one idea or quote that you find interesting or challenging or helpful. Briefly share whatever you selected with the group.

Option 2
What comes to mind when you hear the word *imagination*? How do people in our society tend to view imagination? Is it taken seriously or not? Why do children seem to have a more vibrant imagination than adults?

Follow either option by asking someone to read the following focus statement:

Whether we realize it or not, our imaginations are always being shaped by key stories that tell us what is real and what matters. We need to cultivate a missional imagination by listening to and submitting to the right story—the biblical story of a triune God on the move. Three key practices help us renew and shape our imaginations for mission:

- When we enact God's story in worship, we glorify God and are shaped into a missional people.
- When we read the Bible for spiritual transformation and find ourselves in the story, we are changed and shaped for mission.
- When we pray, God's power in the world is unleashed in us.

By God's grace, the right story transforms us. We begin to see the world differently. We see from a missional point of view how God is present and active among us. And we are able to imagine the bright future God intends for all creation, even in the midst of darkness. But we've got to tell the right story. That makes all the difference.

Bible Study *(20 minutes)*

Read the following Bible passages, then discuss as many of the questions as time permit. If you can only discuss one of the passages, our suggestion is Colossians 1:15-23.

Activity Variation

You may want to divide into three small groups, with each group taking one of the following passages, then reporting to the larger group.

- Genesis 1:1, 26-2:3
  What does this story say about God? About the world? About us?

  How does this story provide an alternative storyline to the competing stories in our culture?

- John 1:1-14
  How does this story connect with Genesis 1 and 2?

What does this story say about God? About the world? About us?

How does this story provide an alternative storyline to the competing stories in our culture?

- Colossians 1:15-23
  Paul's aim in this letter is to provide an alternative story to the young, struggling church in Colossae who lived in the shadow of the sprawling Roman Empire. The dominant storyline of the day insisted that the emperor was the image of the divine and that the powerful military, thriving economy, and superior culture of the Romans was the key to bringing peace and prosperity in the world (*pax Romana*). In this story Paul tells about another king and another kingdom.

How does this story connect with the above passages of Scripture?

What does the story say about Jesus? About the world?

What does it say about the way of peace and flourishing in the world? What does it say about us?

How does this story counter the Roman story of the way the world is? How does this story counter so many competing stories in our own culture today?

Discussion *(15 minutes)*
As time permits, discuss some or all of the following questions, or use questions raised by group members.

1. The reading for Day 1 says that a "missional imagination" determines our capacity to see God's presence and activities among us. Where do you see God present and active in your life right now? Where do you see God present and active in the life of your church?

2. What is the relationship between worship and mission? What attitudes toward worship characterize the culture of your

church? How does your worship tell God's story (or where does it fall short)? How might you change your worship to make it more effective in shaping a missional imagination?

3. "The Bible reads us just as much as we read it. It makes something of us more than we make something of it" (Day 3). What do you think this means? How have you found this to be true in your experience?

4. What is the relationship between prayer and mission? What kind of emphasis does your church put on prayer? What kind of emphasis do you personally put on prayer? What kinds of things keep us from a richer, more intentional prayer life?

5. "So many Christians think that the life of discipleship is about trying harder. . . . But it's not a matter of trying harder. It's a matter of *training* to be like Jesus . . ." (Day 5). Do you find yourself *trying* to live a missional life, or *training?* Of the various practices discussed (worship, reading the Bible, and prayer), which do you feel you need to be more intentional about in your own training program? What other practices have been important in your own missional training?

Closing *(5-10 minutes)*

Option 1

Let the Lord's Prayer shape your group time of prayer. Divide the key lines of the Lord's Prayer among the group (see next page), and have each person jot down some statements of thanksgiving or petition that connects with that line of the prayer. Then go around and pray aloud each phrase of the Lord's Prayer together, allowing time in between for each person to offer aloud his or her prayers that connect with that line.

Our Father, who art in heaven . . .

Hallowed be your name . . .

Your kingdom come, your will be done, on earth as it is in heaven . . .

Give us this day our daily bread . . .

Forgive us our sins as we forgive those who sin against us . . .

Lead us not into temptation but deliver us from evil . . .

For yours is the kingdom, and the power, and the glory forever . . .

Amen!

Option 2

Spend some time sharing personal joys and prayer concerns. Then take turns praying for each other.

Action Options

Group: Small group members often say that the time spent in prayer with the group is the highlight of the group meeting. Like prayer with our families around our supper tables, praying for each other in a small group setting builds our dependence on God and draws us closer together as a group. Here's a suggestion for extending that prayer time into the week after the meeting: Have someone from the group jot down prayer items offered by group members, then e-mail those items to group members to include in their prayers during the week. Participants can contact others in the group via e-mail to share any new prayer concerns that arise during the time between group meetings.

Personal: Here are a couple of suggestions. Feel free, as always, to substitute your own ideas.

Option 1

Develop a "training program" that incorporates some of the key spiritual practices mentioned in this week's daily readings into your daily or weekly rhythm. We always find a way to make time for what we most value. The key is to be intentional about carving out time and then following through. If you'd like to go one step further and learn more about the various spiritual disciplines, consider reading one of the following books: *Celebration of Discipline* by Richard Foster, *The Life You've Always Wanted* by John Ortberg, or *The Sacred Way* by Tony Jones.

Option 2

Be attentive this coming Sunday to how God's story is enacted in worship. Instead of focusing on how it makes you feel or what you get out of the service, focus on how worship shapes you for joining in God's mission. As you leave the sanctuary, ask God, "What kind of person do you want me to be as I go into the world this week? In response to your great love for me, how are you calling me to love both you and my neighbor more faithfully?"

Missional Improvisation

Can I Get a Witness?

Always be ready to make your defense to anyone who demands
from you an accounting of the hope that is in you.
—1 Peter 3:15

So far in this study, we've focused on the biblical drama of a missionary God who is on the move to make all things new in this world (Week 1); looked at what it means to be a missionary people who are "on the move" to join God's mission (Week 2); and explored the kinds of practices that cultivate a missional imagination—so that we can play our part in the drama with joyful freedom and faithfulness (Week 3).

This week's readings focus on missional improvisation. As we find our place in the biblical drama, God's Spirit empowers us to improvise our role for our own time and place. We'll look at the primary activities of faithful missional improvisation.

One of the first aspects of missional improvisation is *evangelism*—one of those words author Kathleen Norris refers to as "scary religious words." For many of us, even the mention of the word causes our blood pressure to skyrocket. We cringe at the notion of forcing ourselves into a mold that doesn't fit—standing on street corners or knocking on doors. Or we immediately focus on our fears and inadequacies: *I don't know enough about the Bible* or *I'm not a very good Christian*.

Paul mentions *evangelism* as one among a whole list of spiritual gifts (Ephesians 4:11). This means that not everybody has the spiritual gift of evangelism; God hands out these gifts of grace according to his will. But even if we'll never be another Billy Graham, all of us are empowered with the Holy Spirit and called to bear witness to our faith. We need to be ready, says Peter, to tell people the reason for the hope we have.

Saint Francis of Assisi is credited with saying, "Preach a sermon every day. Use words only when necessary." Our actions speak louder than words. If our lives don't bear witness to Jesus, then our words are empty and powerless. On the other hand, if we speak only with our actions and never with words, then people won't know why we live the way we do. The Bible insists that people come to faith not just by seeing the gospel acted out but by *hearing* the gospel proclaimed (Romans 10:14). At some point we must also *talk* about our faith.

Isn't it true that you have faith today because someone—or some people—took the time to speak to you about God? Somebody walked into a Sunday school class or climbed into a pulpit or sat at the break table or held on to you during a really bad time in your life and talked with you about their faith. You heard God's voice in their words. You heard their testimony, and something changed you, something came alive.

I prefer the words *witness* and *testimony* over evangelism. These two words are borrowed from a court of law. Those who are summoned to witness are called upon to tell the truth, the whole truth, and nothing but the truth about what they have seen and heard. It is not our job to convince someone about the truth of Jesus or to change a person's heart. That is the Holy Spirit's job. We are simply witnesses who take the stand and give honest testimony about what we've seen and heard. "I don't have all the answers," you might say, "but let me tell you what I've seen and heard in my own life. This is how I've experienced the presence and power of Christ. This is why I believe."

As you give testimony, remember that Jesus has already been at work in this person's life. And Jesus will continue to work long after we leave. You are likely part of a long chain of people God will use to testify to his love and grace. Some people till the soil, Paul writes, others plant the seed, still others water the seed, and some enjoy the harvest (1 Corinthians 3:5-9). We can never be sure where we'll be in the process of planting and nurturing a seed of faith.

Earlier we noted that an incarnational model of ministry emphasizes *relationships*. While God can certainly use all manner of ways to give testimony, God often works most powerfully in the context of relationships. As we nurture relationships with others and love them for who they are, and not as a mission project, we will be amazed at the natural ways God creates opportunities for us to testify to the hope we have.

The Truth, the Whole Truth, and Nothing but the Truth

*Words kill, words give life;
they're either poison or fruit—you choose.*
—*Proverbs 18:21,* The Message

Yesterday's reading talked about our calling to do missional improvisation by giving testimony about the way Jesus has changed our lives. Today we'll take that a step farther. Giving testimony is much more comprehensive than simply talking about our faith. It has to do with the way we use our tongues in *all* our speaking. The goal is not to wear our faith on our sleeve but to weave it into the fabric of our everyday garments. All our speech must rise from the wellspring of faith.

Testimony is about *telling the truth, the whole truth, and nothing but the truth.* When we use our words to tell the truth in any and every context, we are using our tongues to honor God and participate in God's mission. But let me temper this a bit. It's not just about telling the bare-knuckle truth—it's about using our words to speak the truth in love.

Whenever we use our words to join in God's mission—to build up, heal, forgive, confront in a loving way, set things right, advocate for justice—we are faithful witnesses of God's kingdom. This too is testimony—our words participating in the life-giving, restoring, justice-making Word of God.

In her memoir *The Whisper Test,* Mary Ann Bird tells of the power of words to bless or destroy. Bird was born with multiple birth defects: deaf in one ear, a cleft palate, a disfigured face, a crooked nose, lopsided feet. As a child, Mary Ann suffered not only these physical impairments but also the ridicule of other children.

One of her worst experiences at school was the annual hearing test. The teacher would call each child to her desk. As the child covered first one ear and then the other, the teacher would whisper a phrase like "The sky is blue." Those who could hear and repeat the phrase passed "the whisper test." To avoid the humiliation of failure, Mary Ann would cheat, secretly cupping her hand over her one good ear so she could hear what the teacher said.

One year Mary Ann's teacher was Miss Leonard, the most beloved teacher in the school. Every student, including Mary Ann, wanted to be noticed by her. Then came the day of the dreaded hearing test. As Mary Ann cupped her hand over her good ear, Miss Leonard leaned forward to whisper something.

"Those seven words . . . changed my life," she wrote. "Miss Leonard did not say, 'The sky is blue' or 'You have new shoes.' What she whispered was 'I wish you were my little girl.'"

Mary Anne went on to become a teacher herself. She became a person of inner beauty and great kindness. The turning point for her life was hearing those beautiful words of blessing.

Sometimes the most faithful testimony doesn't sound very religious. A teacher's whisper of encouragement, a word of invitation to a kid who sits by herself in the cafeteria, a word of tenderness to a spouse, a word of interest to an elderly person— all these communicate God's love and grace. Whenever we use our words to join in God's work, our words are never "just" words. They are Holy Spirit filled, God-breathed, kingdom-bringing words that make a difference for the glory of God.

But let's not kid ourselves. Using our words in this way can get us in trouble. People don't always want to hear the truth—especially words that speak to power and injustice and challenge the status quo. And yet God's Spirit gives us courage and boldness to speak the truth, even if it causes conflict or brings persecution. We may trust God's promise that even when the truth is hard for people to hear, speaking truth does set us free.

So let's ask God to teach us to think carefully about our words. Teach us how to speak wisely and well. Teach us how to tell the truth in love. Give us words to speak that will bless and not curse. Give us words that point people to God's in-breaking kingdom.

And let the words of our mouths and the meditations of our hearts—in our homes, neighborhoods, schools, and workplaces—be pleasing in God's sight.

Developing Compassion Permanence: Doing Justice

He has told you, O mortal, what is good; and what does
the Lord require of you but to do justice, and to love kindness,
and to walk humbly with your God?

—Micah 6:8

My youngest daughter, Abby, is nine months old. She has a certain toy that she loves to play with—it lights up, spins, and makes all kinds of noises. When the toy is in front of her, she is mesmerized by it. She reaches out with her chubby hands to touch it. But if someone removes the toy from her sight, she instantly loses interest. She doesn't try to search for it. It's as if the toy never existed.

Infants have not developed the mental capacity for what psychologists call *object permanence*—the capacity to understand that an object exists even when it's out of sight. So for babies, it is literally "out of sight, out of mind."

Adults sometimes lack object permanence too. In his book *Good News About Injustice*, Gary Haugen confesses, "I read about innocent people being slaughtered in Rwanda on page A1 of the *Washington Post*, and I am appalled. But my mind moves on to other things with amazing speed and thoroughness when I read on page D15 that the movie my wife and I were hoping to see actually starts a half hour earlier than we thought" (p. 38).

I have to admit that I'm the same way. And I'm guessing that you are too. We control what we see and how much we see. It's so easy to avert our eyes from the vast injustices in our world.

Of course this ability is perfectly natural—and even healthy. Our eyes can only take in so much. Constantly fixating on all the suffering in the world can be overwhelming, even paralyzing. We don't need to feel guilty because we're enjoying a movie with our spouse, playing with our kids, or heading out for an afternoon bike ride.

In Week 3 we talked about cultivating a missional imagination, which at its heart consists of a new way of seeing. Doing missional improvisation also requires us to develop a capacity for what Haugen calls *compassion permanence*—the capacity to remember the needs of the world even when they are out of our sight. But more than just *remembering* the needs of those who suffer injustice, missional improvisation calls us to *act* on their behalf to change their situation.

Jesus is our example of what it means to develop and act on compassion permanence. He was always seeing the people who were invisible to everybody else—those spurned by others as "the last and the least." Jesus showed them compassion and dignity.

In Matthew 25:31-46, Jesus calls us to enact justice on behalf of those who are oppressed and downtrodden. True faith, he says, always shows up in acts of compassion and justice. If we are not feeding hungry people, giving drink to those who thirst, sheltering homeless folks, clothing those who have no clothes, visiting prisoners—if we are not caring for people who are poor and broken, we have to wonder if we have true faith. "Faith by itself, if it has no works, is dead," says James matter-of-factly (James 2:17).

But then Jesus says something even more striking. Not only are we called to act justly on behalf of the last and the least, but Jesus is mysteriously present among those who suffer. "Just as you did it to one of the least of these," Jesus said, "you did it to me."

We must not to fall into the trap of thinking that justice and compassion are a one-way street. Because what we discover when we go to those "in need" is that Jesus is already there! He was there long before we arrived, sharing in their suffering. So when we go to "do ministry" with someone in need, we often come away feeling blessed because we also *receive* Christ's ministry.

How's your compassion permanence? How informed and mindful are you of those who are suffering in our world? In your own community? Who are the invisible people you brush by each day? Will you tilt your head and squint your eyes to see Jesus in them? Will you enact justice on their behalf and reach out to them in their place of need?

Note: If you'd like to learn more about seeking justice for others in your community or the world, visit these and other websites: The Christian Reformed Church: www.crcna.org; Reformed Church World Service: www.rcws.rca.org; International Justice Mission: www.ijm.org; Evangelicals for Social Action: www.esa-online.org; Sojourners: www.sojo.net; and World Vision: www.worldvision.org.

The Artist in All of Us: Creating and Delighting in Beauty

One thing I asked of the Lord, that will I seek after: to live in the house of the Lord all the days of my life, to behold the beauty of the Lord, and to inquire in his temple.

—Psalm 27:4

I remember vividly the day Tammy and I went to look at engagement rings. The jeweler showcased for us a whole display of lovely rings. But what really made those rings beautiful to us, especially the ones we picked out, was the promise to which they pointed—a life together.

In a similar way, we must acknowledge that what is most beautiful about God's world is not the way it is right now but the promise of what it *will* be when God's kingdom has fully come.

Our Creator is a God of beauty. And being created in the image of God means that we too are creative. The first task God assigned Adam in the Garden of Eden was naming the animals—an act that made Adam a co-creator and drew on his God-given creativity. Then God gave Adam and Eve the mandate to be fruitful and multiply—a call to create that goes far beyond childbirth. Today God invites us—the church, God's missionary people—to join in the mission of creating and delighting in the beauty of God's redeemed creation, a future that is already breaking into the present.

When we think about what it means to be witnesses of the risen Christ, most often we think first of evangelism and justice. But this third aspect of faithful missional improvisation—creating and delighting in beauty—is just as important as sharing our faith and doing justice.

Many of us don't think of ourselves as artists. We can't draw or paint. We never acquired a taste for poetry or the ability to play a musical instrument. We don't like to act in the theater. And of course it's true that God has created and gifted some to be artists in these particular ways. However, being created in the image of God and re-created in Christ makes all of us artists! Each of us has the impulse and the capacity to create, and to find joy in doing so. So even if you never play the violin or read Emily Dickenson or apply paint to a canvas, you are called to join God's mission by working to bring forth beauty in this world.

How do we do that?

Perhaps for you being an artist means planting and tending a garden or being a good steward of the environment. Perhaps it means cooking or building something out of wood. Or maybe you exercise your artistic impulse when you rearrange your living room, design a website, write a letter, or tell stories to your kids or grandkids. All these and more arise from our God-give, impulse to create. We are acting missionally when we use our creativity not only for ourselves but to serve God's world.

Most of us will never forget where we were on September 11, 2001. The following day, still in shock, I attended the morning chapel service of a Christian college. I remember jostling through the crowd of students, trying to make my way into the sanctuary amidst all the chatter and clutter.

Then something beautiful happened. Against the backdrop of all the dissonance, faintly I could hear the pure soaring melody of a single violin playing the hymn "It Is Well." As the chatter subsided and students began to make their way into the sanctuary, I closed my eyes and leaned back to listen. Tears streamed down my cheeks and peace settled in my troubled mind.

This is the power of art. In a broken world, at its very best, art speaks to our souls and gives us a window into God's hopeful future.

As we saw in Week 1, the last act of the biblical drama will not end with God destroying this beautiful world, still in the grip of sin. God intends to renew the whole creation. And that new creation is bursting forth *now*. So we join God's mission by celebrating, creating, and enjoying the beauty that glorifies his name. We reflect the artistic heart of the Father as we wait for the day when all of creation is redeemed.

Radical Hospitality: Making Room for Others

*Do not neglect to show hospitality to strangers, for by
doing that some have entertained angels without knowing it.*
—*Hebrews 13:2*

Jeremy was in his early twenties. He was on his way to a job
interview, and he needed some gas money to get there. So
we drove a few blocks to the gas station, pulled up next to
the pump, and Jeremy's car guzzled down gas like a parched
dog lapping up water from a puddle.

At the pump, Jeremy and I got to talking. He'd been taken
away from his mother when he was four years old. He spent the
next thirteen years bouncing from one foster home to another
until he was old enough to be on his own, with no family
connections.

The gas pump let out a loud click, and Jeremy gave the
handle a couple more squeezes to make sure the fuel tank was
full to the rim. I wished him well and turned around to pay the
cashier. Jeremy grabbed my arm. "Hey, wait!" he said. "You're
a pastor, right? Let me ask you something. See, I've made some

stupid mistakes, really messed up bad. But I'm trying to get my life back together, trying to change some things."

I nodded and listened.

"What I was kind of just wonderin' is . . . Is there a place for somebody like me in your church?"

Caught off-guard, I fumbled my words. "Well, yeah, of course," I said, trying to sound confident. *Would they?* I wondered. *Would they really accept Jeremy? Somebody so different from them?*

Five years later, Jeremy's question still haunts me.

Hospitality is a wonderful word that describes the idea of "making room for others." It's a theme that runs through the entire Bible. These days we may associate hospitality with entertaining guests with the creativity and charm of a Martha Stewart. But that's not what the Bible means by it.

The Greek word for hospitality is *philoxenia*, which combines the word for love for people who are connected by kinship or faith (*philo*) and the word for stranger (*xenos*). True hospitality is showing compassion toward the stranger. Welcoming and making room for others. Providing for the physical needs of others, including food, shelter, and clothing. Recognizing a person's worth and dignity.

Hospitality is at the heart of missional improvisation. Since God has welcomed us in Christ, Paul reminds us, we who were once strangers because of sin must now welcome others. He challenged the early believers to "pursue" hospitality—even specifying hospitality as a key qualification for church leaders. Radical hospitality was—and still is—one of the clearest and most compelling marks of the church. All the walls that divide us—race, class, status, culture, gender—are brought down in the blood of Jesus, and we are united as one family in Christ.

Let's think practically about what it means to practice radical hospitality as those who follow Jesus in mission. It means we're called to embody grace by opening our arms to receive others.

What if we viewed our homes as "mission outposts" in our neighborhoods—places of hospitality that welcome others in Jesus' name? What if we resisted the powerful current of a busy lifestyle and slowed down enough to make room for relationships, especially with people who are different from us? What if we befriended someone who feels disconnected and lonely? What if we taught our kids to seek out those who are not popular?

What if disciples of Jesus were *known* for how well we welcome others with grace and love? What if our congregations were *known* as communities with a place for all the Jeremys in our world?

David Kirk describes hospitality as a sacrament of God's love in the world. A sacrament of God's love. That's what it means to be missional!

Discussion Guide

Opening *(10-15 minutes)*

Option 1

Invite the group to tell about an experience you had where God gave you an opportunity to improvise in the moment. Or maybe it was a surprise conversation or a sudden opportunity to show Christ's love. What happened? How did you respond to the Spirit's promptings in the moment? What became of it?

Option 2

Glance back through the five daily readings and choose one idea or quote that you find interesting or challenging or helpful—or a question or comment you have about one of the readings. Briefly share it with the group.

After either of the above options, read the following focus statement:

Faithful missional improvisation involves playing the notes of testimony, truth, justice, beauty, and hospitality in a million and one variations. It happens after hours of practice (spiritual disciplines) when we are open to the leading of the Holy Spirit in the moment. While we have our script—God's story revealed in the Scriptures—to guide us, we don't have a script or a musical score for what's going on in our lives right here and now. But we do have the Holy Spirit. As we surrender to the Spirit, the very presence of Christ works through us to bring about God's healing and renewal in the world.

Bible Study *(15-20 minutes)*

Read Acts 10:1-48 and answer the following questions.

- How is Peter being called to do missional improvisation? Which of the various aspects of improvisation—testimony, truth, justice, beauty, hospitality—can you find in this story?
- What do you think Peter's vision means?
- What is the element of surprise in this story? What does the Holy Spirit do in the moment that challenges Peter's (and the Jewish Christians') assumptions?
- How do you think the Holy Spirit wants to challenge our assumptions today? Where do you see the Spirit doing fresh things that may go against "the way it's always been"?
- What other biblical examples of "missional improvisation" come to mind? You may want to check Luke 9:1-17 and Acts 8:26-40 for two familiar examples.

Discussion *(20 minutes)*

As time permits, discuss some or all of the following questions, or use questions raised by group members.

1. "Fear, not ignorance, is the real enemy of evangelism" (Rebecca Manley Pippert, *Out of the Salt Shaker and Into the World*). Talk about some of the fears group members have about sharing their testimony. What accounts for these fears? How can we overcome them?

2. Read the paragraph in the reading for Day 2 that begins, "Sometimes the most faithful testimony doesn't sound very religious." Then describe a time when a fellow Christian's words meant a great deal to you.

3. What suggestions do you have for developing "compassion permanence" (Day 3)? What are some ways that you can put that compassion into action in your community?

4. How does your church encourage the arts and embrace creativity? If it is lacking, why do you think this is? How might you help change this?

5. How is your church community going beyond just being friendly to *embracing* others?

Alternate Approach

Page back through the readings and review the five aspects of missional improvisation, taking time to solicit reactions and questions from the group. Then, as a group, select one or two of the five aspects from the readings and imagine what it might look like if your church put a greater emphasis on this particular practice. For example, let's say you picked "creating and delighting in beauty." What would be different if your congregation more deeply embraced beauty and creativity? How would your worship services look different? How would your facilities be different? What new ministries or programs can you envision?

If you wish, have someone write down the main points of the discussion and share them with your pastor, a staff member or lay leader, or the appropriate team or committee in your church.

Closing *(5-10 minutes)*

The best jazz musicians say that before they play the music, the first and most vital activity is to listen. They *hear* the sound before they play it. The same thing is true with missional living. We must always listen to the Holy Spirit before we improvise. The Holy Spirit gives the directions and empowers us to speak and to act in just the right moment.

Spend some time together in silence, just listening. It may be a bit uncomfortable, but allow the silence to stretch long enough for you to truly listen. Then, out of your listening, offer the prayers that the Holy Spirit puts on your minds and hearts as you seek to do faithful missional improvisation in your individual lives and congregations.

Action Options

Group: Consider learning more about the needs in your own community and then think about how the group can advocate justice for those who suffer. Maybe the group is already doing this by taking on a service project, as suggested in the Action Options for Week 1. If not, consider having the group participate in a project like Habitat for Humanity, serve in a local soup kitchen, or write letters to political leaders about a justice issue.

Personal: Here are three suggestions from which to choose (or use your own ideas):

Option 1

One of the most effective ways for us to give testimony is to share our faith story. Everyone has a faith story, and every faith story is exciting, regardless of how "undramatic" you think it is. Take some time to write out the story of your faith journey. Here are some questions to get you thinking:
- When did Jesus become real to you?
- Which people were influential in your journey?

- Which significant circumstances or events mark your journey?
- Why do you believe in Jesus? What difference has he made in your life?

As you write your testimony, imagine you are responding to a friend who asks why you are a Christian. You may want to come up with a one-minute testimony and then a longer option (four or five minutes) so you can choose which is best for the amount of time you have to share. Rehearse your statement, perhaps with a spouse or close friend, and use the feedback to make improvements. Consider taking time in your next meeting to share everyone's testimony with the group. It's good practice!

Option 2

Think about the people in your life who are unbelievers or seekers or on the edge of faith. Think in term of family, friends, neighborhood, workplace, extracurricular activities, clubs, and organizations. Make a list of five people you will commit to praying for.

Option 3

Ask God to help you identify someone who lacks friendship and connection, and then make room in your life for a relationship with this person. Invite her out for coffee or a meal. Practice seeing her as an imagebearer of God. Listen to her story. Think of ways you can recognize her value and dignity. If she does not know Christ, pray that God will use this friendship to draw this person into his saving grace.

Finding *Your Place* in the Story

Here Am I, Lord: Answering God's Call

Then Mary said, "Here am I, the servant of the Lord;
let it be with me according to your word."

—*Luke 1:38*

The speaker was a wealthy businessman at a conference. "To be honest," he said, "one of my motives for making so much money was simple—to have the money to hire people to do what I don't like doing. But there's one thing I've never been able to hire anyone to do for me: find my purpose and fulfillment. I'd give anything to discover that" (told by Os Guinness in *The Call*).

Every single one of us is on a search for significance. We yearn to find and fulfill a purpose bigger than ourselves. We want our lives to count for something.

Each of us has a unique role to play in God's story of redemption, and our hearts long to figure out exactly what that role is. This last session will help you explore how God is calling *you specifically* to live a missional lifestyle.

The word *call* is often used to describe the vocations of pastors and other church types. But the truth is that God is in the business of calling each one of us, including you. *You* have a calling—or perhaps even multiple callings.

The word *vocation* comes from the Latin word *vocatio*, which literally means "voice calling." The Bible is chock full of these vocational moments—stories of how ordinary people are minding their business and then, unexpectedly, God calls out to them. It may not be an audible voice. For the prophet Elijah, God's call didn't come in the wind or the earthquake or the fire but in a still small voice from within. Likely this is how it is for most of us.

When God called Abraham on that starry night to be the father of God's covenant people, he was a very old man, almost too dumbfounded to speak. And when his wife, Sarah, heard the news about her own call—her barren womb would be the source of all the nations' children—she burst out laughing. Moses responded to his call to tell Pharaoh to let God's people go by arguing with God that he wasn't the right guy for the job. But God wouldn't be talked out of it. God put an end to Moses' protests with these words of promise: *I will be with you.*

In my favorite of the Bible's "call" stories, the angel Gabriel appears to Mary and announces that she's going to have a baby who would be called *Emmanuel*, which means "God with us." I admire Mary's response. After her simple question, "How can this be?" the angel assures her that nothing is impossible with God. And she simply accepts the call. Just like that. "Here am I, the servant of the Lord; let it be with me according to your word."

In addition to our *primary calling* as followers of Jesus, each of us has a *specific calling*. That means the way in which we live out our identity as disciples who join in God's mission will look different for each person. Some of us are called to live missional lives as mechanics or executives, others as nurses or teachers or stay-at-home parents. Author and teacher Quentin Schultze refers to all these specific ways our primary calling is lived out as "stations."

Take a minute now to think about all the different "stations" in your life where this missional identity is lived out. These include your job, relationships, geography, and other circumstances. A list of my stations, for example, might look something like this: child of God, husband, father, son, brother, pastor, friend, neighbor. I could go on to list specific situations in my life right now where I sense God is calling me to be part of his work. What would your list look like?

God calls all of us to find our place in his story. Sometimes the specific "stations" we're called to may catch us by surprise. God may call us to do something that we never would have thought of or regarded ourselves as qualified to do. But when we, like Moses, begin to offer a litany of excuses, God gives us the same enduring promise: *Do not be afraid. I will be with you.*

However the call unfolds, however difficult the path gets, the Lord will be with us. And this promise gives us the courage and the joy to say, "Yes, here am I, Lord. Let it be with me just as you have said."

The Art of Paying Attention

There the angel of the Lord appeared to him in a
flame of fire out of a bush; he looked, and the bush
was blazing, yet it was not consumed.

—*Exodus 3:2*

Yesterday's reading reflected on how every single one of us receives a calling—or multiple callings—from God. Our primary calling, made visible in the waters of baptism, is the same for everyone: to follow Jesus. But each of us is also called to specific "stations" where we live out our identity as missional Christians. The remaining readings will help you begin to discern what your own "stations" may be.

We'll start with the art of paying attention.

My daughter Emma likes to crawl up in my lap when I'm sitting in my favorite chair. She'll often try to talk with me, even if I'm immersed in a good book or focused on the evening news. And if I'm not listening, she'll take her little hands and turn my face toward her and say, "Dad, you're not paying attention to me!"

I wonder how often God says the same thing to us. "You're not paying attention! You're so busy and so easily distracted that you're not seeing what I'm doing in your life right now!"

The art of paying attention has to do with the capacity to slow down, to avoid the bombardment of distractions, and take notice of what God is doing in us and around us. It is to be stirred with a holy curiosity and wonder.

One of the best-known and beloved stories about calling is the story of Moses in Exodus. Moses, tending his father-in-law's sheep, leads the flock beyond the wilderness to the mountain of Horeb. There angel of the Lord appears to Moses in a flame of fire out of a bush. Moses *looks*—he notices this strange sight— and then he draws closer to see what's going on. And then God calls out, "Moses! Moses! Come no closer! Remove the sandals from your feet, for the place on which you are standing is holy ground" (Exodus 3:4-5).

We often think of the burning bush as an obvious and dramatic way for God to get Moses' attention. But I suspect this burning bush was much more subtle than we tend to think—in the vast open desert, even a bush crowned with flames would be easy to overlook in the midday glare of the scorching sun.

That's our clue: the burning bush in the story was subtle enough to ignore but strange enough to pique the curiosity of someone who was paying attention. Only *after* Moses sees the bush and draws near in wonder does God call out. Moses' capacity to pay attention actually *precedes* the moment of hearing God's call.

If we are going to discern God's call so that we can find our own place in God's story, we need to learn this art of paying attention. The Bible teaches that God is sovereign. That means nothing in our lives happens by sheer chance, and we must be careful not to discount or dismiss anything. God may be trying to get our attention through the smallest of ways.

Sometimes "burning bushes" come in the form of circumstances that invite our curiosity. *How strange*, we think. *I wonder if God is trying to tell me something through this?* Or maybe the burning bush comes in the form of a need that sparks your interest or grabs your heart. Or in the form of another person who points out potential in you that you didn't see in yourself.

In my own discipleship journey, "burning bushes" often come in the form of "interruptions." My response to interruptions tends to be frustration at what I think is keeping me from focusing on my ministry. And yet, the gospels show that Jesus' best ministry often happens in the interruptions—when he's on his way from here to there, intending to accomplish this or do that. Jesus is never in a hurry. He always has time to turn aside and see the burning bush.

This isn't to suggest that every rock you turn up results in a call from God. But why not be curious? What do you have to lose? Wonder about the things that catch your attention. Slow down enough to catch your breath and take a closer look. You might find yourself standing on holy ground.

Maybe *You're* the One You've Been Waiting For!

"I have observed the misery of my people who are in Egypt;
I have heard their cry on account of their taskmasters. Indeed,
I know their sufferings, and I have come down to deliver them. . . ."
—Exodus 3:7-8

Several years ago I heard Bill Hybels, the founding pastor of Willow Creek, give an unforgettable talk on the question "What motivates people to take up a cause and give themselves wholeheartedly for its sake? Why do these people do what they do?"

People work to make a difference, Hybels concluded, because they've been seized by a "holy discontent." He went on to remind us of a popular cartoon character from the 1930s. Popeye was a short, bald sailor with abnormally large forearms, one eye pinched shut, and a corncob pipe sticking out of his mouth. Every cartoon featured the same basic storyline: Popeye's girlfriend, Olive Oyl, would fall into danger (most often at the hands of the villainous Bluto). At some point Popeye's blood pressure would boil and he'd blurt out the words, "That's all I can stands!" He'd squeeze open a can of spinach and swallow the green lump in one single gulp. Instantly infused with superhuman strength, he'd snatch his precious Olive Oyl from the jaws of danger.

Occasionally we may have our own "Popeye moment"— moments when we're confronted with a reality that breaks our heart, gets our blood boiling, and ignites a fire in us. Like Popeye, we may reach the end of our fuse and say, "That's it! I can't stand this any longer! Something needs to change!" Moments of holy discontent like these can help us discern our unique place in God's story.

Moses was born of a Hebrew woman but adopted as an infant by Pharaoh's daughter. One day the grown-up Moses wanders out and sees how the Hebrews are being mistreated by their Egyptian captors. After watching an Egyptian violently beat up a Hebrew slave, Moses snaps. He kills the Egyptian and then hides him in the sand.

The next day Moses goes out again. This time he sees two Hebrews fighting with each other. It's bad enough that his people are being oppressed by the Egyptians, but now things are so bad that they're turning on each other! This is the breaking point for Moses. He's had enough. Something needs to change. When Moses confronts the Hebrews, they say, "What are you going to do? Kill us like you killed the Egyptian?" Afraid, Moses flees to the land of Midian.

Moses runs away, but he can't escape the holy discontent stirring in his heart. God had lighted a fire in Moses' heart long before his encounter with the burning bush.

What kind of fire is God stirring in your heart? Where is your holy discontent? What breaks your heart? What makes you angry when you see it? Pay attention to the righteous anger that compels you to do something in the face of injustice.

Instead of just complaining (which we're all prone to do), or waiting for someone else to come along and do something about it, consider that God may be calling you to be an agent of change. As Christian activist Jim Wallis put it, maybe *you* are the one you've been waiting for!

So often our greatest ministry arises out of our deepest pain. God has a way of using our own tragedy and heartache to become a ministry of blessing to others. A man who goes through cancer encourages others whose lives are turned upside down by this illness. A woman who goes through a divorce walks alongside other women who are struggling in their marriages. After we experienced the pain of not being able to have children biologically, God turned our sorrow into joy by blessing us with two beautiful little girls through adoption. Today, one of our most passionate mission "stations" is to walk beside others who are struggling with the same thing. I'm guessing it's the same for you. God often uses our pain to stir our hearts and join God's ministry to others.

Wherever it comes from, pay attention to that "Popeye moment." The temptation will always be there to look the other way or to suppress that holy discontent. But pay attention. Instead of squelching the fire, stir the embers and fan the flame!

Maybe this is God's way of helping you find your unique place in his story. Maybe you really are the one you've been waiting for!

Feeling God's Pleasure: Doing What You Were Made to Do

" . . . to one he gave five talents, to another two,
to another one, each according to his ability. . . ."
—*Matthew 25:15*

The movie *Chariots of Fire* tells the story of a Scottish Olympic runner. Eric Liddell loves running, but his long-term plan is to go to China to be a missionary. In one memorable scene, Eric's sister, Jenny, worries that his desire to compete in the Olympics is deterring him from his higher calling to the mission field. Eric says to her, "Jenny, God has made me fast. And when I run, I feel his pleasure."

We've explored how we may discern God's call when we pay attention to the burning bushes that happen around us and within us and how God's call is often linked with our holy discontent and to our deepest pain. But we must also pay attention to what gives us joy. When we're pursuing what God calls us to, at some level we should experience God's pleasure and delight in us. And in our joy, God is glorified.

My wife and I have known Dylan Perez since he was a boy. Our families became good friends at church. It's been a joy to watch Dylan grow up and mature over the years. What has been most exciting has been to watch him discover that thing that God created him to do—play the piano. Now a freshman in college, Dylan is one of the most talented pianists I know. I love watching Dylan play the piano because I can see him feeling God's pleasure as he leans in with his eyes closed and gets lost in the music. Dylan feels most alive when he's playing piano. And he brings life to others as he glorifies God and blesses them with his incredible gift.

What brings you joy? Do you engage in some kind of activity that makes you feel alive? That energizes you so much you lose track of time? That you'd do even if you didn't get paid for it?

Finding pleasure in an activity or cause is a good indication that it may help you find your place in God's story. But enjoying something by itself isn't enough. You also need to develop skill. Dylan didn't just enjoy playing the piano—he also worked hard at developing his talent.

So the next question to ask is, What are you good at? What kinds of roles and activities have others affirmed you in? Where do you feel like you can make the greatest contribution, given who you are and how God has made you?

The church staff I'm a part of has adopted a strengths approach to ministry. Instead of focusing on improving your weaknesses, a strengths approach is based on the idea that people find the most joy and make the strongest contribution when they are building on their strengths. No doubt God can work through our weakness, but it makes sense that we will best discern the ways God is calling us to join him in mission if we identify and develop the talents God has given us.

In Matthew 25:14-30, Jesus told the parable of the talents, which referred to money. Each of the servants received a different amount of talents from their master. Two of the three servants built on their talents, and their master praised and rewarded them. The other servant buried his talent. When his master found out, he rebuked the servant and took the talent away.

Nowhere does this parable (or anywhere else in Scripture) say we are responsible for developing talents we don't have. We are only responsible for developing the talents we've been given. God's expectation is that we will take the talents he's given us and develop them for his glory and in the service of others.

It's wonderful to realize that we may find our place in God's story not merely through obligation, but in those things that give us our deepest satisfaction and pleasure.

Discovering Your Spiritual Gifts

*But each of us was given grace according
to the measure of Christ's gift.*

—*Ephesians 4:7*

So far this week we've talked about discerning God's call and finding our unique place in God's story by paying attention to the burning bushes around us and within us, and by focusing on doing the things we're good at and that give us the greatest joy. Today we'll explore one final avenue of discernment that can equip us for faithful missional improvisation: discovering our *spiritual gifts*.

The church, as we've seen, is not the place where we go on Sundays. It's not a religious shopping mall for filling our spiritual needs or an exclusive club with perks for its members. *We* are the church, the living body of Christ—one body with many parts.

"There is one body and one Spirit," writes Paul, "just as you were called to the one hope of your calling, one Lord, one faith, one baptism, one God and Father of all, who is above all and through all and in all" (Ephesians 4:4-6).

This call to unity, however, does not mean we're all the same. It is not a call to colorless uniformity or bland sameness. As one body with many parts, God has gifted us with remarkable diversity in personality, temperament, skills, perspectives, and experience. And diversity in *spiritual gifts*. Paul goes on, "But each of us was given grace according to the measure of Christ's gift."

Of course Paul is referring to the best gift of all, which is the presence of the Holy Spirit poured out at Pentecost. But that is not all we've received. Along with the Holy Spirit, Paul says, Jesus has given each of us *charismata*—gifts of grace.

What are these "gifts of grace"? Paul mentions five in Ephesians 4: "The gifts he gave were that some would be apostles, some prophets, some evangelists, some pastors and teachers. . . ." But this list is by no means exhaustive. Other New Testament passages list different gifts of grace in addition to these.

In Romans 12:4-8 Paul lists prophecy, service, teaching, giving, leadership, and compassion. First Corinthians 12 includes yet another of Paul's lists, including wisdom, knowledge, faith, healing, discernment, and speaking in tongues and interpreting tongues.

But even all these gifts put together are not meant to be an exhaustive list. Paul's point is that *every* disciple of Jesus, *every* member of Christ's body, has received "gifts of grace." None of us gets left out. Spiritual gifts are gifts of grace because we do not apply for them or earn them, nor are they given based on who God favors most. They are special abilities given purely according to God's will and purposes.

What's the purpose of all these gifts? They're not for ourselves alone. And certainly not so we can show off or boast or push our own agenda. Paul makes it crystal clear that these gifts have been given for *the common good* (1 Corinthians 12:7). They're intended "to equip the saints for the work of ministry, for building up the body of Christ" (Ephesians 4:12).

Have you discovered your spiritual gifts? Do you know what "gifts of grace" Jesus has given you so that you can build up Christ's body and join God in mission? How are you developing those gifts and exercising them?

In my first parish there was an elder who was famous for always saying, "God doesn't put square pegs in round holes!" His point echoes the apostle Paul's teaching about spiritual gifts. God doesn't call us to do something he hasn't first provided the spiritual resources for. The key to finding your unique place in God's story and doing faithful missional improvisation is to discover your spiritual gifts and put them to use for the glory of God.

When that happens, you'll be contributing to the shared mission of the body of Christ—and experiencing joy and fulfillment.

Discussion Guide

Opening *(10 minutes)*

Begin by listening as each person in the group has the opportunity to share a helpful thought, inspirational insight, or question that arose from the daily readings. Don't have a discussion yet—just practice the art of paying attention!

Then ask someone to read the following focus statement aloud:

As disciples of Jesus, God has given us his mission to give focus and meaning to our lives. Each of us has the same primary calling to follow Jesus and to join God's mission in the world. But God also calls each of us to play a unique role in God's story of redemption by living out our primary calling in very specific ways. These specific callings are different for each of us. We can discern our unique role in God's story by looking at the "stations" in which he's placed us (for example, in our relationships, geography, and circumstances), paying attention to the "burning bushes" around us, listening to our holy discontent, discovering our strengths and what gives us joy, and identifying our spiritual gifts.

But even as we seek to find our unique place in God's story, we must keep in mind that God is always the main actor on this stage. Even as we join in God's mission, it is always about who God is and what God is doing. The point of finding our unique role in God's story is never to draw attention to ourselves but always to make our lives reflect the light of God's glory.

Bible Study *(20 minutes)*

Read Exodus 3:1-15; 4:1-5, 10-16. Then use the following questions to lead your discussion.

- Why did God require Moses to first turn aside and take notice before God addressed him?
- What does this teach us about the ways in which God may be trying to address us in our own lives?
- How does Moses initially respond to God's call (Exodus 3:11)? Why do you think he responded this way? What are some of the similar excuses we use today?
- How does God respond to Moses (verse 12)?
- Moses asks God who he should say has sent him, should the people ask. What name does God give Moses to share with the people (verse 14)? What do you think this means?
- In spite of God's promise to be with him, in spite of additional signs, Moses still isn't ready to say yes to God's call (Exodus 4:1, 10). What can we learn from this about who God calls? About our own call to participate in God's mission?
- Is there anything else that strikes you about this passage that has to do especially with the notion of being called by God?

Additional Bible Study (Optional)

If time permits, take a look at the story of Timothy's call (2 Timothy 1:1-14). One of the dangers of thinking about God's calling is to presume that it always has to be dramatic, as in the case of Moses or Paul. Timothy's calling emerged from a quiet and stable life of nurture in the Christian faith by his grandmother Lois and his mother, Eunice. What does Paul instruct Timothy to do (1:6-7)? How does one "rekindle the gift of God that is within you"?

Paul also instructs Timothy to not be ashamed of the gospel, nor to be ashamed of Paul himself. Why do you think Timothy may have been tempted to be ashamed? How are you tempted to be ashamed of the gospel today?

Discussion *(20 minutes)*

Discuss some or all of the following questions as time allows, or discuss other questions group members have about the daily readings. If you take question 5, below, you may want to drop or limit discussion of some other questions so you'll have enough time to respond thoughtfully.

1. What do you think of as being your "calling" from God?

2. Can you think of a time when you sensed God calling you to be or do something that you felt at least somewhat unqualified for? How did you respond? Looking back, what did you learn from that experience? Why do you think God has a habit of calling people who feel they're not the right ones for the job?

3. "So often our greatest ministry arises out of our deepest pain" (Day 3). How has this been true in your experience or in the experience of someone you know?

4. "The place where God calls you is where your deep gladness and the world's deep hunger meet" (Frederick Buechner). How has this been true in your experience or in the experience of someone you know?

5. Share with the group one or two specific ways you sense God is calling you to live out your unique place in God's story, to

put your strengths and spiritual gifts to work in his service. How did you come to discern this? In what ways are you still struggling to discern your unique place in God's story?

Alternate Approach

Instead of using the above questions, spend the remainder of your time together writing personal mission statements that articulate your best sense of who God is calling you to be and what he is calling you to do. Make it as clear as you can, but keep in mind that this is a first draft—you can polish and refine your statement at home this week.

Here's one way you could begin your statement: "The reason I exist is to . . ." To give you an idea of what a mission statement could look like, here is author Brian Keeper's statement:

I am not my own but I belong to God in Jesus Christ. Therefore, I exist to know God and be known by God; and also to glorify God by participating in his mission to manifest his kingdom in the world. The primary ways God has called me to participate in his mission are, first of all, by daily surrendering my life to Christ's lordship; second, by loving my wife and daughters and letting our family be a sign of God's kingdom; and third, by leading a local congregation to be a sign of God's kingdom. In leading a local congregation, I will invest myself most fully in developing leadership among the consistory, the staff, and emerging leaders in the congregation.

Take time to share your mission statements with the group, even if the statements are in rough form or incomplete. Get some feedback from each other. You can also share completed statements by e-mail this week, if you wish.

The goal in refining your personal mission statement is to write it on your heart and let it give your life focus and direction as you set priorities and make daily choices.

Closing *(5-10 minutes)*

As you come to the end of this study, take time to pray for each other as group members seek their unique place in God's story and live a missional lifestyle. Go around the group and share personal joys and concerns. Ask everyone how the group can specifically pray for them.

Action Options

Group: Consider having an extra meeting to share and provide feedback for either personal "testimonies" developed by group members as a follow-up to last week's session or personal mission statements (if not done as part of the Alternate Activity in today's session). If an extra meeting isn't practical, group members can use e-mail to exchange either of these two personal responses.

Personal: Here are several ideas for following up this session:

Option 1

If you haven't already done so in today's session, write (or refine) your personal mission statement at home this week (see Alternate Activity under "Discussion" for details). If you wish, share your statement with group members by e-mail or at an additional meeting. If you'd like more help in writing a personal mission statement, read the *Focused Living Retreat Workbook* by Terry B. Walling and Gary Mayes (http://leaderbreakthru.com) or *Purposeful Living* (a unique resource used in the RCA; contact Ken Eriks at keriks@rca.org or Rodger Price at rprice@rca.org). As you gain clarity on how God is uniquely calling you to join him in mission, take the next steps to act with obedience and faithfulness.

Option 2

Using the questions embedded in Day 4, identify your top three to five strengths. Consider asking some others who know you well what they see as your strengths. Once you discover your strengths, be intentional about building on them (as opposed to focusing on your weaknesses). An excellent resource for identifying your strengths is the Gallup StrengthsFinder. This web-based survey is designed to give you immediate feedback on your top five strengths as identified by your responses to its questions. If you wish to take the StrenthsFinder, purchase a copy of *StrengthsFinder 2.0*, which contains instructions that will help you access the instrument so you can complete the survey.

Option 3

If you haven't discovered your spiritual gifts, complete an inventory that helps you identify them. One such inventory can found at www.elca.org/evangelism/assessments/spiritgifts. html. Another good source is *Discover Your Gifts and Learn How to Use Them* by Alvin J. VanderGriend (FaithAliveResources.org). Once you've discovered your spiritual gifts, or if you already know them, commit to at least one way of using these gifts to build up Christ's body and join God in mission. Continue to discern the unique way(s) God is calling you to live a missional life by finding your place in God's story of redemption.